PENGUIN BUSINESS
SILVER LINING

Kamal Shah was diagnosed with kidney failure in July 1997. He has been on dialysis ever since. He got a kidney transplant from his mother in 1998 that did not work out. Despite being on dialysis for more than twenty-five years now, Kamal leads a completely normal life. He works, travels, exercises and has fun. He believes that anyone on dialysis can lead a normal life provided they get good quality dialysis. He co-founded NephroPlus, a dialysis centre network, in 2009, which enables dialysis patients to lead completely normal lives. NephroPlus is now India's largest dialysis centre network and is also present in three countries beyond India. Kamal has a widely read blog about his journey on dialysis: www.kamaldshah.com.

Celebrating 35 Years of
Penguin Random House India

ADVANCE PRAISE FOR THE BOOK

'Kamal Shah, a dialysis patient himself, refused to let his disease defeat him, instead using it as a source of inspiration: how could he prevent others from suffering as he had? It was this focused mission that gave rise to NephroPlus, a story Shah tells deftly here'—Shashi Tharoor, member of Parliament

'Be a silver lining in someone's cloud—this book does more, much more than that. Every sentence hangs heavy on one's heart really. What an amazing eye-opener this book is. Just as you start wiping your tears away, comes a lovely positive paragraph. A must-read for everyone. For you and I who knew nothing about this topic and are still groping, this is a must. Kamal Shah is a person one can fall in love with just by reading about him and his passion. Every chapter is both informative and clinical. And at the same time, just the right amount of emotion. "I Had a Dream" and "The Winner Takes It All" just did it all for me. If you care and love, then this is the book for you. Informative, passionate, emotional and a learning experience. I wish Kamal Shah and all his endeavours nothing but the BEST. God bless'—Usha Uthup, singer

'Reading Kamal Shah's book does convince you that while no one consciously seeks setbacks, if one should happen, you can take a creative leap forward. Almost like a visionary, Kamal Shah asserts that NephroPlus dialysis guests (not patients) should radiate positive energy and be strong in the self-belief that they can lead a full and normal life. Kudos to the concept and the story'—R. Gopalakrishnan, author and business commentator

'Recovering from health issues that typically cause people to give up on life, Kamal Shah went on to set up a patient-centric healthcare company that continues to grow from strength to strength. This book chronicles the entire journey and is a must-read for all'—Madhu Mantena, film producer

Silver Lining

Overcoming Adversity to Build

NEPHROPLUS

India's Largest Dialysis Provider

Kamal Shah

PENGUIN
BUSINESS

An imprint of Penguin Random House

PENGUIN BUSINESS

USA | Canada | UK | Ireland | Australia
New Zealand | India | South Africa | China | Singapore

Penguin Business is part of the Penguin Random House group of companies
whose addresses can be found at global.penguinrandomhouse.com

Published by Penguin Random House India Pvt. Ltd
4th Floor, Capital Tower 1, MG Road,
Gurugram 122 002, Haryana, India

First published in Penguin Business by Penguin Random House India 2023

ISBN 9780143463191

Typeset in Garamond by MAP Systems, Bengaluru, India

www.penguin.co.in

Contents

Contents

Foreword

Eighty-five per cent of dialysis patients in India cannot access dialysis even today! This number used to be 95 per cent about thirteen years ago when NephroPlus was co-founded by Kamal and me. I am deeply obliged to Kamal for being my partner in this fascinating journey of NephroPlus.

I was quite restless in 2008 in the US while working for the blue-chip consulting firm McKinsey. I really wanted to make a dent in the Indian healthcare system but was not able to figure out how. In early 2009, a thesis was emerging in my head that India would need a lot of help in the diabetes and hypertension ecosystem and by mid-2009, I filtered my various ideas into four specific opportunities, one of which was a professionally run, standardized dialysis network across India.

I chanced upon Kamal when a Google search listed his blog as the first result for the keywords 'Dialysis in India'. That evening, I started reading his blog and could not stop until five the next morning. Kamal is a great writer and the way he had shared his experiences around how he started his journey with dialysis and all the adversities he had overcome, I was truly fascinated. I sent him an email and he promptly responded, and we corresponded for a few months. When I moved to India in late 2009, I met Kamal over breakfast the very next day and he was even more impressive in person. While I travelled around India to validate my ideas, the more I saw the way dialysis units were being managed, the more I was convinced that this area needed help. I had a strong view on our USP for NephroPlus. Just Kamal.

When a co-founder is himself on dialysis for twenty-five years, you know that no other company can as truly and as deeply understand customers' pain points, needs and wants as much as NephroPlus. We quickly incorporated NephroPlus in December 2009 and the last thirteen years of this journey have been quite amazing. We have raised two rounds of angel funding and five rounds of private equity, and grew to a network of more than 315 centres in 195 cities spread across four countries.

Kamal knew the challenges that dialysis patients in India were facing due to his personal experience across several hospitals in India. He methodically noted all these challenges and set out to solve them one by one from scratch. As we both were not doctors, we were thinking more like engineers (we both are coincidentally chemical engineers!) to approach these challenges from an 'operations' viewpoint.

One of the biggest challenges that Kamal deeply felt about was cross-infections in dialysis units. Thirteen years ago, 33 per cent of dialysis patients in India were getting cross-infected with hepatitis C, hepatitis B and HIV! Kamal was quite 'angry' that dialysis units were adding the burden of liver disease for patients who were already suffering from kidney failure. We methodically understood various touchpoints in a dialysis unit and came up with a product and a process to eliminate cross-infections in dialysis. We came up with a Zero Infection Point kit (ZIP kit) which would be unique for each of our patients. We also created the RenAssure 56-step process to eliminate cross-infections emanating from various touchpoints. We proudly claimed 'Zero Cross-Infections' at NephroPlus.

Kamal also always hated when people on dialysis were called 'patients'. That gave birth to the golden word 'guest' in NephroPlus. He always thought people admitted in ICUs can be called patients, but people on maintenance dialysis can lead a normal life—they can work, exercise, travel and have fun just like anyone else. From day zero, Kamal banned the word 'patient' at NephroPlus. Everyone in the company, including the super specialist doctors, calls our customers 'guests'. He was also instrumental in ensuring every guest had a dedicated TV set, Wi-Fi Internet and had great power over schedule and modality at NephroPlus. We came up with the idea of the Dialysis Olympiad where hundreds of NephroPlus guests and other patients would come to this event to participate in track and field events and get actual medals. This year, an Olympic medallist, Bajrang Punia, came and presented the medals to all our winners, and you must note that this is the only such event conducted across the world. Kamal loves to travel, and he wants our guests to travel without any inhibitions as well. Hence, we developed India's only holiday dialysis network with beaches, hill stations and various pilgrimage destinations across India!

Kamal also was instrumental in ensuring our core value of 'Guest care comes first' percolates throughout the network. This has become ingrained in our DNA so strongly that every single teammate at NephroPlus lives and breathes this core value. This is visible in almost every single process across the network. For example, Kamal heads quality control and ensures that not a single inferior-quality product enters our procurement system. He keeps telling all the teammates, 'Just make the guest smile and everything else is going to be fine.' Our clinical teammates at the centres genuinely put the guest care aspect ahead of their own convenience and comfort and this is validated by the amazing feedback from guests across the four countries we serve.

Kamal is one of the few people I look up to and get inspired by, every day. He is the main reason why NephroPlus has scaled up to become the largest network in India and is now spread across other countries too. He is our brand ambassador and conscience-keeper. I feel very lucky to be his partner and co-founder at NephroPlus!

14 March 2023

Vikram Vuppala,
founder and CEO,
NephroPlus

Part 1

1

The Dawn That Wasn't

'Deep in the man sits fast his fate
To mould his fortunes, mean or great.'
—Ralph Waldo Emerson

I handed over the papers to the consular officer through the semi-circular opening at the bottom of the glass panel as I waited on the other side. A cold breeze from the air-conditioning on the other side touched my hand. My heart was pounding. My mouth was dry. I could feel a million drops of sweat form on my head. I took a deep breath and tried to relax.

The officer went through the papers, one by one. He looked at my GRE scorecard, then my I-20, and at the end, my college exam memos.

'Counter number four, please', he said. I felt blood rush up all the way from my limbs to my brain. I was being given my student visa for pursuing a master's in the United States (US)! Counter number four was where I had to pay the visa fee. A long saga was drawing to a close.

Images of the past year flashed in my mind. Reluctant at first following a period of disillusionment, I had not written in time to US universities asking them for application forms. On being goaded by my parents and, after subsequently changing my mind, I started asking friends for application forms that were lying unused and applied to those universities. I saw myself waiting outside professors' cabins to request for recommendation letters. After receiving several rejections, I got admitted into the University of Akron in Ohio. What a tumultuous year it had been!

As I was leaving the consulate building that morning of 12 July 1997, I rushed through the greens. At the gate, among the group of family members of other visa applicants, I spotted my father looking at me, trying to figure out what had happened. Worry creased his forehead, reflecting his racing heart. The rest of his face was still not betraying any sign of emotion. I ended the suspense right then. As he saw me signalling with a thumbs-up sign, a smile that conveyed more relief than joy appeared on his face. He burst out laughing.

The anxiety that accompanies the whole visa approval process had not only engulfed me, but my entire family as well. We called home and told my mother that I had got the visa. Those were the days when you still used a landline telephone. My mother muttered a prayer of thanks as soon as she heard the news. To celebrate, my father and I hosted a few folks from our extended family staying in Chennai for lunch at Dasa, a restaurant on Chennai's famous Mount Road. They had the best dosas there.

My father and I took the evening train back to Hyderabad.

When I reached Hyderabad the next day, I started preparing for my move to the US. I made a checklist of things I needed to finish. My mind was racing. I had to cover as much ground as possible within a brief span of time.

The next day, I went to the Institute of Preventive Medicine. I had to get vaccinated against hepatitis B, typhoid, measles, mumps and rubella. This was a standard thing that everyone going to the US did. The building was a shabby, old structure with paint peeling off the walls. The officials talked to me as if they were doing me a favour. I got the vaccines and rushed out of there. They told me there could be some minor side effects.

Towards evening, I got feverish. I put it down to the vaccines.

To celebrate the visa, I started planning a small party for some friends. I had secured the gold medal from our university for standing first in the final bachelor's degree programme in chemical engineering. Winning the gold medal was very special. Until the third year of our four-year programme, I was in fourth place. Various things distracted me in the third year. In the fourth year, though, I got my act together and worked hard. I topped both the semesters by a wide margin and came first in the university exams. I had secured the top spot in my school during Class 12 public exams as well. And now this. I was proud of my efforts.

The next morning, I went to my college where I was to meet up with a few friends and plan the party. I was feeling queasy and attributed it to the vaccines, yet again. This had to be temporary, I told myself.

Temporary it was not. There were unexpected changes taking place inside my body. These changes would alter my life in a manner I could never have imagined. Vaccines cause the body's own defence mechanism—its immune system—to become capable of fighting off a violent infection later.

In my case, the vaccines triggered a chain of events that led to my body's immune system going into overdrive. All control mechanisms of the body that would have kept the immune response to the vaccine in check, failed.[1]

My kidneys started failing, little by little. Within twenty-four hours, I had lost about 80 per cent of my kidney function. Toxins and fluids that the kidneys typically flush out were being retained in my body. Fluid started accumulating in various areas.

Oblivious of the turmoil within, I booked my tickets for the US. I would leave in two weeks.

* * *

By the evening of the third day following the vaccinations, the nausea had worsened, and I started throwing up. To rule out anything serious, we went over to our family doctor, Dr Kirit Parekh. My aunt, who is a doctor, was also involved in the discussion by then. They got a few tests done.

We knew the doctor at the lab. When we went over to collect the results, he asked me to wait outside and called my father and aunt inside.

When they came out, I asked them what was happening. They said there was a problem with my kidneys. We went back to Dr Parekh, who studied the reports with a grim face and suggested that we consult a nephrologist, a kidney specialist. My serum creatinine was 7.0 mg/dL. The normal range is 0.5 to 1.2 mg/dL. I had no clue what that meant. Something temporary, I thought. Some medicines would fix it.

We fixed up an appointment with a nephrologist, Dr Girish Narayen, who had been recommended by Dr Parekh. We went to meet Dr Narayen at Hyderabad's Medwin Hospital.

Medwin was a very large, multi-speciality hospital in Hyderabad's Nampally area. It was a good forty-five-minute drive from our house. Since the hospital was located within a commercial complex that housed several shops and offices, it was very noisy all around. After we paid the consultation fee, they asked us to wait outside Dr Girish Narayen's outpatient department (OPD). The waiting area had no natural ventilation, only artificial lighting. This made it quite depressing. There was a mild disinfectant-like odour as well. After waiting for about half-an-hour, they asked us to go inside.

Dr Narayen was a tall, fair and bespectacled middle-aged man. Around fifty years old was my guess. His combed hair with a set pattern gave the impression that he had applied gel or oil just a few minutes back. After completing his MBBS and MD in general medicine from Osmania Medical College, among Hyderabad's most reputed medical colleges, he completed a Doctorate of Medicine (DM) in nephrology from Post Graduate Institute (PGI) in Chandigarh in 1982. PGI Chandigarh was one of the best medical colleges in the country. He had about fifteen years of experience in nephrology and about twenty years of expertise as a doctor.

Dr Narayen looked at the prescription from Dr Parekh and then asked me to lie down on the examination table. He put his hand on my stomach and felt it at different points. With his fingers, he checked my ankles. To feel different points on my chest, he used a stethoscope.

Most doctors say 'Deep breath' when they want to hear sounds from your chest or back. Dr Narayen, who had seen thousands of patients in his career, just said, 'Hm . . .' I figured he wanted me to take a deep breath, so I did. 'Hm,' he went again. I took another deep breath. Another 'Hm,' another deep breath.

He asked me to check my weight on the weighing scale he had right next to the table. It showed 76.1 kg. While he went back and sat on his chair, I sat on the stool beside his table. I would need a few more blood tests. He also asked me to restrict my fluids to a litre a day. I wondered how much water I drank daily. Since I had no clue then, I wondered if one litre was enough for a day. He added that I would need a kidney biopsy. My aunt let out an 'Ah', her eyebrows arching upwards in disbelief.

Sensing my aunt's shock, Dr Narayen said that we needed to know what the reason for the decline in kidney function was. He suspected it was a disease called atypical haemolytic uremic syndrome (aHUS) but he needed to confirm it and for that, a biopsy was the only solution. I had no clue what a biopsy was. Dr Narayen asked me to get admitted to Medwin Hospital the following day.

That evening, my extended family came by to check on me. I was quite weak by then. I slowly walked down the steps from my room on the first floor. I made sure I was smiling all the way down. I did not want anyone to worry about me. I was sure I would be fine in a few days. My uncle remarked that I looked fine and cheerful.

It was the first time in my life that I was being admitted to a hospital. My room was mid-sized. There was one large window on one side, which looked over other buildings that were full of offices. The window ensured that the room was well-lit and it would be bright the entire day unless you drew the curtain. The view wasn't inspiring at all. How beautiful can old office buildings be?

Dr Narayen came to see me and said that I would need a dialysis session. I had never heard the word until then. Wondering what it meant and what the procedure would feel like, I just hoped there would be no pain.

The staff soon wheeled me to the hospital's dialysis centre on the fourth floor. They asked me to lie on a bed next to a machine. The machine was a little bigger than a washing machine. It had strange lights, some of which were going on and off. Every once in a while, the machine would beep, startling the newer patients in the centre. The experienced ones were used to it by then. The hospital staff would come and press a button and the beeping would stop. I did not like the look and sound of the place.

As I looked around me, I saw several other beds with people lying on them. There were similar machines near their beds. The patients were old and miserable. I felt like a hare that had walked into an enclosure meant for tortoises in a zoo.

Soon, a doctor joined me. He asked my family to wait outside the unit and then checked my weight and blood pressure and noted them. After selecting a point on my thigh and cleaning it, he said that I would feel some pain as he was giving me a small injection. I wondered why he had to give it in my thigh.

I felt a needle. It stung.

'Ttttsssssssssssss . . .'

'Finished. Finished.'

After a few seconds, I felt him putting a bigger needle inside my thigh. The pain this time was quite bad.

'Aaaaahhhhhhhh . . .'

'Relax. Relax.'

In a few seconds, I saw blood flowing through the pipes connected to the machine and realized that it was my blood.

The session was violent. I felt nauseous and signalled to the doctor that I needed to vomit. They brought what they called a kidney tray, which I used. I was also asked not to move my leg as the catheter, which was being used to draw and return the blood, was in my thigh and moving the leg would dislocate it.

The session lasted two hours. When the doctor removed the thick needle inserted in my thigh, he closed the site with thick gauze and tape, which had to be held for an hour to prevent it from bleeding.

As they took me out of the dialysis centre in a wheelchair into the elevator and up to my room, I tried to take my mind off the entire episode and looked around me. A lady who looked like she was in her mid-fifties was with us. As we got into the elevator, she asked my mother, who was with me, 'First dialysis?'

'Yes,' my mother answered.

'You also had a session?'

'Yes, this was my ninety-fourth.'

My eyebrows arched in horror. How could anyone suffer this trauma ninety-four times?

* * *

They had planned the kidney biopsy next. They needed it to find out the actual cause of decline in kidney function. Dr Girish Narayen thought it was aHUS because this disease is associated with three symptoms that I had—anaemia (low blood counts), thrombocytopenia (low platelet counts) and uraemia (compromised kidney function), but it was important to confirm it. This would dictate the future course of treatment.

For the biopsy, the hospital staff took me to a room next to the dialysis centre. They asked me to lie on my stomach. Dr Girish Narayen himself was to do the biopsy. He administered a local anaesthetic. He then inserted the biopsy gun (the needle that would extract the tissue) in what was a painful process despite the local anaesthetic. It was also very uncomfortable as you needed to lie in a position that enabled easy access to the kidneys that are located in the back of the body. They got pieces of tissue out and sent them off to the lab for analysis.

Dr Narayen asked me to lie on my back and not move for the next twenty-four hours. This was very uncomfortable. When they don't give you any such instructions, you may not end up moving anyway. But when they ask you not to move, you feel like moving again and again.

While we waited for the results of the biopsy, which would take a week, a urologist, Dr Mohan Raj, who happened to be my brother Prasan's friend's father, created a shunt[2] in my left arm. This would give easy access for dialysis instead of the painful thigh-based access.[3]

The second dialysis session was painless thanks to the shunt. It lasted three hours and was much better compared to the first one.

The biopsy result came back inconclusive as they could not get actual kidney tissue. In those days, biopsies were like putting your hand in a box full of marbles of different colours and being asked to pick out the red one. You had marbles in your hand but would just have to take a chance on the colour.

Dr Narayen decided to request a senior nephrologist, Dr J.C.M. Sastry to see me and review my case. Dr Sastry had recently moved to Hyderabad's Kamineni Hospitals and was very knowledgeable. Since this was a complicated case, Dr Narayen wanted to get a second opinion. We went and saw Dr Sastry and showed him all the reports.

'It's Acute Tubular Necrosis (ATN),' he decided with an air of confidence.

'How many days would it take for the kidney function to recover, doctor?' I asked.

'My own research says seven days,' he thundered.

That didn't sound too bad. In another two or three days, I should be fine, I thought.

There was a fundamental disagreement between the two nephrologists. While Dr Sastry thought it was ATN[4] that had affected my kidney function, Dr Narayen felt it was aHUS.

When we met Dr Narayen again, we figured he had already discussed this with Dr Sastry. But he was sticking to his own diagnosis. He had thought this through and was going with aHUS!

While this meeting with Dr Sastry was a brief one, he would play a very large role in my life a little in the future.

They planned dialysis every three to four days depending on my blood tests. I was also asked to measure my urine output every time I peed.

Published research on aHUS around that time stated that plasma exchanges and even infusions would help in aHUS.[5]

So, at almost every dialysis session, they also gave me fresh frozen plasma from a donor. I also received plasma exchanges where they infused donor plasma and removed part of my body's plasma. I also needed several blood transfusions to bring my blood counts to normal. All this would need several blood donors. To make things worse, my blood group was O negative, which was a rare blood group. Donors were difficult to find.

My father's old friends from his Lions Club days, Inderchand Jain and Muralidhar Rao, took charge of the entire blood donation drive. They did various things from releasing ads in newspapers to putting together a list of donors to be contacted from various sources. They would also coordinate the complete process from picking up the donors and bringing them to the hospital, and getting them to complete the donation process and then dropping them back. The strangest thing was that I did not meet the two of them even once during my hospital stay. Behind the scenes, with no hullabaloo, they took away a major source of stress from my parents' minds. These are things you never forget.

Dr Narayen made another attempt at a biopsy after a few days. This failed as well. He then moved me to another hospital where they could do a biopsy under the guidance of an ultrasound machine, which would enable a more accurate extraction of kidney tissue.

This was a famous hospital in Hyderabad's Jubilee Hills area. Dr Narayen had spoken to Dr Krishnan who was a nephrologist there. Dr Krishnan was a little junior to Dr Narayen. He had done his MBBS and MD from Delhi University and then a Diplomate of National Board (DNB) in nephrology from Hyderabad's Osmania University.

Dr Narayen would come to the hospital as well for the biopsy, though he did not regularly practise there. Dr Krishnan made me feel comfortable as soon as I spoke to him. Warm, affable and cheerful, he would always be ready with a one-liner to lighten the sombre mood.

The room, though, was not as airy and bright as the Medwin room. The only light you got was from the tube light in the room. There were no windows. I did not like that at all. Being in a hospital was bad enough. Being stuck in a room with no ventilation made it worse.

The procedure was the same except that they were using the ultrasound scanning device, which had a probe that was being moved around my back, to stream hazy images of what was within. These images helped Dr Krishnan to guide the biopsy needle into the right place. He got kidney tissue, which he sent to the lab for analysis.

That evening, I had severe pain. It felt like someone had plunged a dagger in my back. I was crying. My father rushed to the nursing station to tell them about the pain. No one responsible was there. He went from desk to desk trying to reach out to someone who could help, but only a nurse was available who did not have instructions to administer anything. My aunt who was with us told the nurse that she was a doctor and asked her to administer a powerful painkiller. Putting her job on the line, and moved by the sight of me crying out in pain, the nurse did as she was told. The pain subsided in minutes.

However, clots had begun to form in the urinary tract, which would not allow me to empty my bladder. I tossed from side to side. The doctors concluded that the biopsy caused an injury to the kidney which had bled and clots had formed all the way down. Urologist Dr Mohan Raj was called in, who decided that a cystoscopy[6] was needed.

So, they moved me to the operation theatre at the hospital and performed the cystoscopy. The procedure was painless but uncomfortable, which I did not mind. Thankfully, the passage had cleared, and I could pee freely then.

The biopsy result was conclusive. It was atypical haemolytic uremic syndrome. This was a very rare disease that affected about two to three per million people around the world. Dr Girish Narayen was right about the primary disease.

They discharged me from the hospital and asked to come for dialysis to Medwin Hospital.

* * *

Haemolytic Uremic Syndrome can be typical or atypical with different symptoms, outcomes and types of people affected.[7] All this categorization has been more recent. When I was diagnosed, very little was known and everyone assumed my kidney function would recover. That was not the case.

During every dialysis session, I would ask my doctor about when the kidneys would revive.

'It's very close now, Kamal. Maybe another week.'

'You said that last week too.'

'Yes, I know, but it's difficult to predict this accurately.'

The routine went on.

'A few more days.'

'A little more time.'

'One more week.'

I was getting restless. How long was this routine going to continue? It was more than a month since this ordeal had started. We were not doing anything different. How would the results be any different?

All this while, I assumed that it was a matter of a few weeks. Once I recovered, I would book my tickets and leave for the US to get on with my life. Things did not seem to be improving. What was the next step?

When I was not recovering from the trauma of a dialysis session, these thoughts kept bothering me. I was fed up of waiting for my kidneys to revive on their own.

In September 1997, my doctor decided to try a course of steroids. He had probably read about it in some journal. I don't know for sure. He wanted to put me on prednisolone because he wanted to try something different. He was not sure if it would work. Since it had been close to two months and there was no sign of the kidney function improving, he had to do something new. So, he started me off on the steroid.

Within a few days, my kidney function started improving. The volume of urine, a direct indicator of kidney function, started increasing on a daily basis. Within a couple of weeks, things seemed to have gone back to normal. We were all very excited.

The events of the last few months had seemed like we were lost in a forest with no sign of being able to find our way out. Dangers lurked at every corner. We didn't know how to get out. Then, we tried something random. It looked like we had hit upon the right path to get out.

To celebrate, one Sunday evening, my parents, brothers and I went out for dinner. It was after a long time that we were having fun. We were an ordinary middle-class family staying in Secunderabad, the modern twin of Hyderabad, the 400-year-old city in the Deccan Plateau of south India. My father, Dilip, was a businessperson whose ancestors were from the village of Anjar in the Kutch district of Gujarat and had migrated to Bengaluru (then Bangalore) several decades ago in the hope of prosperity. My father was born to Mohanlal Parekh and Sarojben Parekh in 1951. The family moved to Hyderabad when he was a teenager to set up a branch of their business in film distribution called Jagat Pictures. It soon became the most reputed film distribution company in the city. Our family is staunchly Jain. My grandfather was the president of the Jain Sangh of Secunderabad while my grandmother was the president of the Mahila Mandal (women's wing) of the same Sangh.

My father worked, for most of his life, in Jagat Pictures. When film distribution became a risky business and revenues were on the decline, the family decided to shut down the company. After my maternal grandfather's passing in 1994, my father started managing his bookstore and newspaper agency, and also a clothing store in Secunderabad. He retired in 2016.

My mother, Archana, was born Ava Fernes to Byron and Gladys Fernes in 1954 in Hyderabad. My maternal grandparents were Goan Christians. Heading the Hyderabad office of a multinational company called Mekaster, my grandfather also acquired a famous bookstore called J.C. Pinto on Secunderabad's Mahatma Gandhi Road and ran a newspaper distribution agency from the same store. My grandmother was a senior doctor and a visiting consultant to two air force stations in Hyderabad. She also had her own private practice in Secunderabad and ran a clinic at home.

My mother worked with Andhra Bank for thirty-three years before retiring in 2014. She loved her work and was dedicated to the bank. She grew fast within the organization and was an exceptional performer. Based on her capabilities, the management appointed her as the manager to several branches, one by one, and she exceeded her targets almost every time. She was passionate about her work, and whatever she took on, she excelled in it.

My parents met and fell in love when they were in the Leo Club, the youth wing of the Lions Club, the social service organization. Their marriage in October 1974 created quite a stir within their respective families. A Gujarati Jain marrying a Goan Christian in a yet-conservative India in 1974 was difficult to imagine. The families did not accept the relationship at first, but over time, they did. My birth in September 1975 was one reason that the level of acceptance improved.

My two brothers, Prasan and Karan, were born three and eight years after me, respectively. All three of us completed our schooling from Hyderabad Public School in Begumpet, the city's most reputed educational institution. While I chose chemical engineering, Prasan and Karan did their graduation in commerce.

Prasan is now the proud owner of Stone Plus, a company that purchases natural stones from quarries and exports them to several countries, with his largest clientele based in the US. Prasan married Anjali, though they now stay separately. They have two beautiful children, Naman and Nidhi.

Karan works at AT&T in Los Angeles (LA) in the US as a business analyst. He did his MBA from Pepperdine University in LA. He is married to Myra, an occupational therapist whose parents are originally from Taiwan.

This kidney disease brought something challenging to our close-knit family, which had only my parents, my two brothers and me at the time. We had to face it with courage and determination. We had hardly had any fun time together since the diagnosis. Our Sunday celebration was the perfect opportunity to get some relief from the recent drudgery.

We went to a restaurant that was quite far away from home. We ordered our favourite dishes, and laughed and joked. The last several weeks had taken quite a toll on all of us. This was the break we all needed. It looked like our troubles were all ending.

On the way back home, it started pouring. As my father made a turn at a crossroad, a vehicle that was passing by drove into a puddle of water. Since I was sitting by the window, I felt the water on my face first. I rolled it up with a start, wary of catching any infection. Since I was on steroids, I had a compromised immune system.

By the next morning, I had caught an acute lung infection. My aunt came home. She spoke to Dr Girish Narayen, who asked me to come and see him. I went back to Medwin Hospital. He did a quick evaluation and admitted me. He did not want to take any chances. After all the uncertainty, he had revived the kidneys and wanted to do everything possible to avoid a relapse. He put me on some basic antibiotics. However, even after a couple of days, things had not improved. The lung infection was becoming worse. Dr Narayen decided to consult with a pulmonologist.

Both the doctors discussed the situation at length. There was a dilemma at hand. On the one hand were the recovering kidneys and on the other, the infected lungs. It was almost as if they had to choose one pair of organs from the two. If the doctors treated the lung infection aggressively, they could lose the kidney function that had improved after considerable effort. If they did not, the lung infection could turn serious, endangering my life.

Clinically, the choice was straightforward. They had to treat the lung infection. Lungs are more critical for survival. They used a 'sulfa drug' called Bactrim and started me off on a high-strength dose.

Within a day, the lung infection started getting better. Bactrim was the right drug for the infection. As expected, my kidney function deteriorated. My urine output started reducing. Every morning, my lungs would get better and my kidney function further declined. The doctors were helpless. There was nothing they could do. They could just watch. Within a week, my lungs had recovered completely while my kidney function had gone back to a stage where I needed dialysis.

We were back to where we began.

All it took was one storm, one possibly flawed decision of going out to celebrate a major victory in this battle with kidney disease. Who knows how things might have turned out if we hadn't ventured out that evening? Should we have been more cautious? The doctor hadn't advised us to stay indoors. So why should we have not gone?

Again, was the lung infection a result of the water splashed on me? We can never be sure. Though chances are that it was the cause, we can never say this without doubt. Bacteria and viruses are such tiny little beasts that you can never pinpoint where, why and how an infection was contracted.

Often, the infection happens much before its symptoms manifest. This is true for both bacterial and viral infections. So, one can never say for sure that a particular incident caused it. This makes preventing an infection a matter of chance. Often, people are exposed to harmful microbes for days without getting infected. There are also several times when someone gets infected with only the slightest hint of exposure.

This uncertainty makes treatment challenging. People often berate doctors for not treating them in an accurate manner. But medicine is not an exact science. The complexities of the human body and confounding factors such as this make diagnosis and treatment very subjective. It is not always straightforward.

The brief exhilaration we experienced on our evening out gave way to despondence. I started feeling I might not make it in time for my master's course at Akron. I realized it could take a few more months. While all my classmates started flying out of the country one by one, here I was, bound to a hospital bed.

Just a few months short of turning twenty-two, however, I still had an air of invincibility about myself. I was not going to be deterred by a small obstacle. I thought about the next steps. While fall was the most common semester to start attending a master's course in universities in the US, spring beginnings were not rare. I reconciled with missing the fall semester and joining during the spring semester instead, which would begin in January of the subsequent year. That couldn't be too bad.

We should have this sorted by January, I thought. Dr Narayen's 'weeks' turned to 'months'. I started looking up university admissions online for the upcoming spring. I shortlisted a few and started the application process. On one trip to my college to seek letters of recommendation (LoR) from professors, one of my teachers, who had heard of my health condition, had some sage advice to offer. 'Look after your health first. Admissions can wait.'

I reasoned with him that I would be fine soon. This was only a minor distraction.

The professor's grey hair was well-earned. He had seen more of life than I had. From probably only a cursory description of my health condition, he had gathered that it was more than a minor distraction. He knew I had a lot more to deal with than this.

I couldn't be bothered with the ominous look he had on his wrinkled face. I had to get the letters out of the way and focus on my essays.

* * *

2

A Charmed Glass of Water

'If any remedy is tested under controlled scientific conditions and proved to be effective, it will cease to be alternative and will simply become medicine. So-called alternative medicine either hasn't been tested or it has failed its tests.'
—Richard Dawkins

During the first six months of my diagnosis, many people called us and told us about how someone they knew was cured of kidney disease by one or another alternate therapy. If it was homeopathy one day, it would be Ayurveda the next. One caller would talk about naturopathy and another would extol the benefits of Unani medicine.

My parents wanted to try every single thing. Each new therapy brought with it a new line of treatment, and along with it, a fresh set of diet restrictions. All promises of a cure were about as successful as those of politicians who have showed the electorate the moon and delivered nothing on being sworn into office.

The acupuncture expert was the one who promised the most. He claimed to have cured a lady who had stopped passing urine. To those in the kidney failure world, mostly, the function of the kidney is linked directly to the amount of urine passed. This person claimed that with one session of acupuncture, she began passing about 250 ml; with the second a litre and, with three sessions, it was Ganga Jamuna!

I didn't aspire to pass rivers of urine. I would have been content with a couple of litres. Someone had to pick the man up in a car from a far-off place every day. He would charge what was then a fortune of Rs 1000 per sitting. The first session got done. No change in urine output. The second session got done too. No change. We finished ten sessions. There was no hint of the promised Ganga Jamuna. We gave up.

Around November of that year, Dr Girish Narayen called us to his clinic and said that he was going out of the country for a month and would like us to be under the care of Dr J.C.M. Sastry who practised at Kamineni Hospital in Hyderabad. It made sense. Since this was quite a complicated disease, it would be better if I was under the care of someone experienced in the absence of Dr Narayen. He was the same doctor whom he had referred us to for a second opinion about the primary kidney disease a few months ago.

Hyderabad's Kamineni Hospital had come up in 1995, and the nephrology department had just become operational that year. Set up in L.B. Nagar, it was quite a distance from our house. It was also in a part of the city that we had rarely visited. We headed out to the hospital the following day. The journey took a good forty-five minutes, but there was very little traffic for most of it. In fact, the last stretch of the road that led to the hospital had vast swathes of greenery on both sides, which made it much more pleasant than the ride to Medwin Hospital that had only buildings, buildings and more buildings along the way.

Dr J.C.M. Sastry, we learnt, was a very senior nephrologist, one of the senior-most in the country. Born in Andhra Pradesh's

Tenali district, he completed his medicine from Bangalore Medical College and his MD in general medicine from the All India Institute of Medical Sciences (AIIMS), which is the most reputed medical college in India. He then joined the Christian Medical College (CMC) in Vellore in 1970 and moved to its nephrology department when it started in 1971. The hospital was famous for the Doctorate of Medicine (DM) programme in nephrology. In 1974, he registered for the programme and completed it. He continued to work in CMC until 1996, a long and distinguished tenure of twenty-five years. Highly regarded by the medical fraternity both in India and abroad, he had several stellar achievements in nephrology and had made several research contributions.

Dr Sastry looked every bit the professor we had heard him to be. Short, bespectacled and balding, he had a strict manner about him, one that would send students scurrying for cover when asked a troublesome question. While everyone feared him for his short temper, he could be funny when he chose to. He developed a familial bond with his patients but refused to suffer their families' questions.

After a thorough examination and going through my reports, we were on our way to the dialysis centre of Kamineni Hospital. It was a much larger hall than the one at Medwin. One side had large windows, which allowed for a lot of light. Green palms adorned the outside. This was quite a change from the drab unit at Medwin. There were only a few dialysis machines on one side with a large nursing station in the centre. We met Dr Dakshinamurthy, who was another nephrologist from Dr Sastry's team.

Young and well-read, Dr Dakshinamurthy looked as if he was in his late thirties. He had a short temper as well. The nurses in the dialysis unit shivered at the sight of the two doctors as they thundered into the unit when something went wrong. They would all have a good time, however, when they were in a jolly mood. It was like one big family.

One thing was for sure. The dialysis unit in Kamineni was leagues ahead of that at Medwin in terms of overall appearance and hygiene. Clinical quality was something I did not understand or know anything about then. To an amateur, Kamineni was as uplifting as Medwin was depressing. Isn't that a good sign for a patient?

Dr Sastry put me on a regular thrice-a-week regimen of dialysis. The only trouble with this hospital was the distance. It made dialysis days hectic as all of us had to wake up early, get ready and go for a session. We usually got back only by around 1 p.m.

My overall health stabilized in a few weeks. While initially I used to take a wheelchair from the hospital entrance to the dialysis centre, after a month, I began walking to the dialysis unit. In the beginning, one of my family members would always accompany me for a session. Eventually, I started going alone with the driver. This was a huge thing. The dependence on a wheelchair and an attendant for dialysis took a mental toll like no other. There was this feeling of being a burden. When I got rid of the wheelchair and could go and come from a dialysis session without anyone accompanying me, I felt much better about myself. My feeling of self-worth increased.

I was used to having a little 'forbidden' food—either half a soft drink or half a glass of fruit juice during my dialysis sessions at Medwin. When I switched to Kamineni, I asked the nurse in-charge if I could have a soft drink. She asked me what I wanted to have. I requested for a Fanta. To my delight, she called the canteen and asked them to send a Fanta. When it came, she allowed me to have the entire 300 millilitres! At times, I debate if it was Kamineni's hygiene that I liked more or the extra Fanta they allowed me compared to Medwin.

I also developed a fondness for watermelon. What it was about the fruit that fascinated me, I am not really sure. I had never been a big fan of watermelons before my diagnosis. Was it the name? I had to restrict the amount of water I drank. Was that the reason I had this craving for watermelons? I began bringing a little watermelon to have during the first hour of my dialysis sessions.

I became associated with watermelons in the dialysis unit. When Dr Sastry would walk through the attendants' waiting area and see someone bringing in some watermelon, he would exclaim, 'Oh, Kamal is here today!'

This entire duration of my treatment at Kamineni Hospital saw my health stabilize. I had to get dialysis, but other than that, there were no major problems. Because of this, I continued to get dialysis at Kamineni Hospital even after Dr Narayen came back from abroad. I remained under the care of Dr Sastry.

As the most eventful year of my life was drawing to a close, I had accepted that my US plans would not materialize. While I did get admission in a few universities for the spring semester, I couldn't have been able to reach by the deadline. There was no planning for alternates this time. I had to put all my energy into recovering. This was not the life I had wanted.

When I was put on dialysis in July, it was supposedly only for a few weeks. Six months had passed since then. I often wondered if there was a way out of this. Was it possible? Or was I condemned to a life without normal kidneys? Dialysis days would be characterized by chaotic mornings, the actual dialysis and then sleeping in the afternoon to recover from the session. On other days, I would while away my time watching television and chatting with family. My mind would often be depressed.

Dr Girish Narayen disrupted the initial inertia by trying steroids. What would be the disruptor this time? What could we do differently? I didn't see the doctors even discussing any options. Everyone seemed to have got into a routine. Dialysis went on. Doctors came to the dialysis unit and went. My family kept up the support. I kept waiting for a miracle.

Hope arrived in the most unexpected of ways.

* * *

It was early January 1998. Hyderabad was seeing the coldest days of the year. Coldest really means a few degrees above 10 degrees Centigrade, not what you would typically call cold in, say, north India. Those living in coastal cities of Mumbai and Chennai would, however, relate to this, as the sea doesn't allow for any extreme temperatures. Despite not having the sea for company, Hyderabad never had extreme cold weather, in my memory.

Those were days when email had not yet invaded our lives. An envelope arrived in the mail when the postman came for his once-a-day delivery. My father received the envelope addressed to him. Hoping to find the sender's name, he turned it. It was blank. He opened the envelope. Out fell a newspaper cutting. Someone had circled an article in the newspaper clip with a pen. It had the picture of a man holding a glass of water. My father took the cutting and lowered himself on to a chair at our dining table as he began reading the article.

It talked about a person, a Dr Gupta, who stayed in Mumbai, who had apparently cured many people afflicted with kidney disease by giving them a glass of charmed water. He had received a mantra from a sage in a forest which, when chanted over a glass of water, had the power to cure kidney disease. The 'course' lasted about four months and several people, it said, had no need for dialysis after that four-month period.

My father did not know what to make of it. He handed over the cutting first to my mother and then to me. One after the other, we read it. We all looked at each other, wondering if it

could be true. The anonymous envelope and the magical feel of
the promised cure made for an interesting combination.

Could this be it? By then, I was very frustrated with the events
that had shaken my life and spoilt all my plans. I had resigned
to long-term dialysis and was busy dealing with the day-to-day
problems that kidney disease brought. I had no time to even think
about the future.

The next few days witnessed a flurry of activity and animated
discussions at home. We called my extended family over for
deliberations. Everyone thought there was no harm in trying this
so-called treatment. It was water, after all. My aunt and her family
stayed in Mumbai. I could stay there. I could undergo dialysis at
Jaslok Hospital, which was close to her house. Only till I needed
it, that is. The magic water would anyway get the kidneys to work
soon, right?

We showed the newspaper clip to Dr Dakshinamurthy.

'Defies science,' he reacted after reading the article. 'We have
no problem if you try it,' he added. He said he would let Dr Sastry
know. His face wore an expression of cockiness. It almost said to
me, 'Magic? Yeah, right.'

I feared talking to Dr Sastry about it.

Since childhood, I have often cowered in the face of
authoritative figures. I was, at a subconscious level, scared of
people who were short-tempered or had a dominant streak. I didn't
realize what was happening, though. This played out deep down.

We ran into Dr Sastry one afternoon, in the elevator, on our
way out from the dialysis centre.

I sheepishly asked him, 'Did Dr Dakshinamurthy tell you
I was going to Mumbai?'

'Yes, he told me.'

'You're okay with it, right, doctor?'

'Yes, of course. Both Gandhi and Bulchand are my students.'

Phew. Thank god for that. The magic water did not come up. I was wondering what he thought about that. Did he even know I was going for it? Or did he think I was going to Mumbai because I thought the doctors there (Dr Gandhi and Dr Bulchand were nephrologists in Jaslok Hospital) were better?

In India, most doctors hate their patients taking second opinions. Well, not surprising. This, in one way, signals that you don't trust your primary doctor fully. I get it. No one likes to be doubted, especially in a field that is so knowledge- and experience-dependent as medicine. From the patient's perspective, a second opinion gives them peace of mind. This is life that we are dealing with. One wrong decision might ruin it. It is not some trivial matter. However, often, knowledge comes with a monumental ego. The greater the knowledge, the greater the ego. The combination can be deadly.

If Dr Sastry thought I was going to Mumbai to consult better doctors, it would be an affront to his ego. He was one of the most senior and distinguished nephrologists in the country. Why would a patient go to another city to consult his students? So, I hoped Dr Dakshinamurthy had told him about the miracle water. I preferred Dr Sastry laughing about that rather than being hurt that I was going to consult with his students in Mumbai.

The plan was for my dad to fly with me to Mumbai and get me started on the 'treatment'. Then, my parents and other relatives would all take turns to stay with me in my aunt's house for the four-month duration when I would undergo the therapy.

My dad and I took a flight to Mumbai. It was the first time I was travelling out of Hyderabad after my kidney disease had struck.

The very next day after landing in Mumbai, we drove down to Dr Gupta's office. As we made our way through the busy-yet-disciplined traffic of south Mumbai, I could feel droplets of sweat developing on the base of the roots of my hair caused by the humid air.

Dr Gupta's office was in a run-down, almost dilapidated building on the second floor. An old, rickety elevator transported all the patients up to the balcony, where they waited for their turn.

We talked to the folks outside who were waiting their turn to see the doctor. Each one of them knew someone who had benefited. Many of them claimed that they themselves had benefited too. Some said their frequency of dialysis had reduced from thrice a week to twice a week. We were impressed. We asked them what the treatment was. They said he poured out a glass of water, whispered a mantra on it, and then gave it to the patients to drink. That was it. For four months, you had to drink the water and you were supposed to be cured of kidney disease. He gave you a diet chart that you were supposed to follow strictly.

We waited in the balcony outside the doctor's office for our turn, wondering what the future held. The queue was not too long. Each person did not take too much time either. I guess there was nothing much to do inside, was there? How much time did it take to drink a glass of water?

After a while, they let us into the office. The cramped office was full of old magazines, most of them *Reader's Digests*. I wondered if this man was a dealer for *Reader's Digest*. The office was full of papers and books stacked one above the other, with the edges hardly aligned. People worked at desks that looked as if they were a few decades old.

Dr Gupta was not a medical doctor. He was a regular businessman. He might have had a PhD which allowed him to use the title of 'Doctor'. This lent a certain respectability to the 'cure'. Every morning, all his 'patients' would troop in, one by one, to drink this elixir of life.

Words have this habit of taking on new meanings so often. Elixir of life, huh? Water, offered in this dingy Mumbai building, provided hope to the many people that arrived day after day, of being liberated from the torturous treatment called dialysis that had become so entrenched in their lives.

Dr Gupta was a middle-aged, well-built man, always dressed in safari suits. He asked us to sit. My father gave a brief background of my disease. He asked for the blood test reports. He took a quick glance at them. I do not think they mattered at all. It was not as if the quantity of the water or the type of mantra would vary based on the reports. There was only one treatment.

I looked on with utmost respect and faith as the rotund doctor poured out a glass of water, brought it close to his mouth and chanted something into it as we leaned in to understand what he was saying. He then handed the glass to me. I drank the glass of water.

Dr Gupta then handed us a photocopied chart with diet restrictions, and a recommended meal plan. I had to avoid pulses. A good part of the remaining instructions were similar to the regular kidney disease diet that one is prescribed. I wondered about the combination of the 'mantra' and a diet chart. If it was the mantra that was doing the trick, what role did the diet have to play? Did Dr Gupta get the diet chart as well from the sage in the forest? It all seemed to be weird. But when you are in this kind of situation, you don't use logic. You simply do what you're being told. And that's what I did.

I left the place full of hope that the four-month journey that I had set out on would be the end of all my problems.

Next, we met Dr Bhupendra V. Gandhi, a nephrologist at Jaslok Hospital.

I had to continue dialysis until the water showed its effect. We were quite upfront about why we were there. The doctor knew about Dr Gupta and his water therapy. Nor did he comment on its efficacy and neither did we ask him about it. He put me on dialysis twice a week, five hours each time.

I got into a routine. Every morning, after getting ready, someone would drive me to Dr Gupta's office. The doctor would pour out a glass of water, chant his mantra over it without anyone else hearing, and I would gulp down the water. On Sundays, we would go to his house, where he would repeat the same ritual.

Dialysis would be twice a week. And each time, it would be five hours of unadulterated torture. I could hardly wait for the miracle-inducing water to act.

* * *

Rita *faiba* (aunt) was my father's sister. I stayed in her home in Mumbai's Chitrakoot Apartment, which was atop Altamount Road. My aunt, her husband, Mukesh, and their two sons, Tanay and Malay, were a very loving and cheerful family. My uncle Mukesh was a diamond merchant from a reputed family business known as Devraj Nensee and Company. They had offices in Mumbai, Hyderabad and Chennai and had established a flourishing diamond business. The family had also got into granite exports and had grown that business well too.

My paternal grandmother, Sarojben, had also moved to Mumbai. I was her favourite grandchild. She would always be there to comfort me, to look after me and to ensure that my every need was taken care of.

Everyone in my family called her 'Bhabhi', which translates to sister-in-law. Her own kids, her daughters-in-law, her son-in-law and all her grandchildren. Every single person related to her in any manner called her Bhabhi. It so happened that my father and his siblings were almost the same age as some of their uncles. Since their uncles would call her Bhabhi, the name stuck and her children also began calling her Bhabhi. This trend continued, and even her grandchildren called her Bhabhi.

Bhabhi was a staunch Jain. With a very sharp mind, she was adept at memorizing the scriptures and was a firm believer in the theory of karma. Widowed in her early forties because of a road accident, she did a brilliant job of bringing up her four sons and daughter. She was very well-respected in our local religious 'sangh', which was a common group of Jain families in the area and had a temple as the centre of all religious activities. The sangh appointed her president of the Kunthunath Mahila Mandal, which was the ladies' wing of the group that performed various rituals for families on different occasions.

I shared an excellent relationship with her and respected her knowledge of religion and worldly affairs.

In Mumbai, Tanay and Malay looked after me like one would take care of a child. I shared an especially close relationship with Malay, my little cousin. We used the term *golmaal* for cheating on fluid intake. I had to restrict my water intake to one litre per day. My aunt would fill up a one-litre bottle with water and I had to drink only from that bottle to ensure that I did not go above the limit.

Like all other dialysis patients, I would cheat when no one was looking and drink water from the fridge or an earthenware pot. Malay would see me doing it sometimes and would warn me saying I could get into trouble. I would dismiss him saying that nothing would happen.

The dialysis regimen was very different in Mumbai. Against the four hours every session and thrice-a-week schedule that I was used to in Hyderabad, I was going for five-hour sessions twice a week in Mumbai. Not only was the number of hours per week lesser than the Hyderabad regimen, but the gap between two sessions was also longer. This was a sure-shot recipe for disaster. Many of my fellow patients were on the same schedule. Despite the agony of the extra hour each session, I liked the fact that I had to do only two sessions every week.

Bombay's Jaslok Hospital was very well equipped. The lead technician, Suresh, was very experienced and adept at his work. The rest of the staff was also very good. One thing I liked about the Jaslok Dialysis Centre was that they served a hot meal during the session. While it was nowhere close to gourmet food, it was a welcome change from the routine food prepared at home. More than the taste, I would look forward to what was going to be served and the whole routine of eating that took away a good thirty to forty-five minutes off the five-hour session.

My uncle loved going on long drives. I loved to travel as well. Every Sunday, we would all head out to some place, typically a place on the outskirts of Mumbai or at least a couple of hours away and spend time there before returning in the evening. If it was Sanjay Gandhi National Park one week, it was all the way to Matheran the next week. One week it was the Aarey Milk Colony and another, it would be Kalamboli. These breaks offered me a chance to get away from the boredom of the daily routine of doing nothing much that I had become accustomed to in Mumbai.

One Sunday, all of us went to a new temple, a couple of hours away from the city. The sun seemed to have forgotten that it was January and was blazing as if it was the middle of summer. I ended up drinking quite a lot of water that day. By the time we returned, I was quite tired. By night, I started feeling uncomfortable. I had difficulty breathing.

We had an oxygen cylinder at home, which I used whenever I had trouble breathing. I hooked on the mask and tried inhaling some oxygen with some deep breaths. That didn't help at all. The breathlessness was increasing with every passing minute.

Within an hour, I was feeling suffocated. It was as if there was no air around me. I was trying to suck in air from my nose. Nothing seemed to go inside. I started panicking. Thinking that I was going to die, I ran to and fro around the room, from the bed to the window and back, looking upward towards the fan and trying to get some air into my lungs. The problem was not the lack of air, of course. The excess water that I had drunk had filled up my lungs. No matter how much air I took in, the lungs could not process it until the excess fluid was removed. I was drowning.

I woke up my grandmother and told her how I was feeling. At once, she woke up my uncle and aunt. They took one look at me and decided to rush me to Jaslok. My uncle called the dialysis unit and alerted them.

We got into the car and headed out. On the way to the hospital, I stuck my face out of the window, trying to get some air. I was struggling to live. The fifteen-minute drive to Jaslok seemed like a never-ending nightmare. Since it was the middle of the night, there wasn't any traffic. But the feeling of suffocation made every moment stretch out into eternity.

Relief arrived with the sight of the board of the hospital. They rushed me in a wheelchair to the dialysis unit and put me on emergency dialysis. The technician set the machine to drain out an enormous amount of water in the first hour. Only then did I feel better. My life slowly came back to me. My breath became less stifled with every millilitre of water that the machine pulled off. As I felt my lungs clearing up, I thought of the couple of hours that had just passed. I felt I had beaten death by a whisker that night. The trauma exhausted my mind and body. I gradually slid into a deep sleep.

That was the punishment I got for drinking water. Not alcohol. Not cola. Plain, simple water. Thirst is a primordial instinct. The cells in the human body crave water when the body gets dehydrated. In dialysis patients, the problem is not that the body is dehydrated. The problem is that water is restricted. When something as basic as water is restricted, the body doesn't learn to cope. It craves water all the time. Only those with tremendous mental strength and willpower manage to overcome this complicated relationship with water.

Switching to biweekly dialysis sessions messed up my mind completely. I had to restrict water even more than before. It had been tough enough before. Now it was worse. I was getting increasingly frustrated. The miracle was not showing any signs of its magic.

* * *

The treatment routine, however, continued. As did the onerous diet restrictions, days filled with nothingness and evenings with my cousins and the family that I would look forward to. One month had passed. There was no change in my kidney function. It was supposed to be a four-month course. I would wonder as to when the water would start acting. If I was to be free from kidney disease in four months, wasn't I supposed to be at least a quarter better in a month?

My family encouraged me to persist and have faith. We would see some results soon. I waited.

The days filled with idle hours spent staring at the ceiling, thinking of what turn my life had taken, weren't helping. I began thinking about whether we were on a futile mission. Was I destined to a life with kidney disease? Should I return to Hyderabad and start planning the next course of action?

An aunt from my mother's side of the family, Anne de Braganca Cunha, believed I should stop this so-called treatment at once. She was sure that Dr Gupta was a fraud and taking people for a ride. Her son, Nikhil, was a radiologist. When an ultrasound scan was ordered to diagnose some breathlessness I was having, the scan revealed a slight increase in the size of the kidneys.

There was jubilation in my family. Normally, the size of the kidneys does not increase if they are failing. My aunt Rita was confident that the miraculous water treatment was working. While there was nothing else like blood values or urine output to show that kidney function was really improving, this was like a brief, passing shower in a drought-hit desert. It did not seem like the showers would help generate a harvest, but everyone still felt happy.

I felt even worse. This false hope meant that I would need to keep at the treatment for longer. I could not wind up and go back and get on with my life. I did not like the boredom and the empty days. I did not like that there was no sure sign of a cure. I wanted to get my life back. I wanted to live a full life again. I started thinking about going back and taking up a job, at least something part-time. My mind was not used to being idle. It needed to be productive.

Around early March, I began talking to my family about giving up and going back to Hyderabad. My family thought I was being impatient and should wait for some more time. They said the only other way out then was a transplant, and that had a lot of other complications associated with it. It wasn't as simple as it sounded.

I argued that I had had enough and was tired of this. Explaining to them that the other factor that influenced my decision was that I was feeling wasted and wanted to do some productive work. I told them I wanted to be busy. In Mumbai, I was idle the whole day. This was not even related to my Mumbai stay. I felt a sense of emptiness within for not doing anything for over six months then.

I was always a 'good boy'. My grandmother called me 'the essence of correctness'. I was the pet of all the elders in the family and of the teachers at school. Conforming to every norm, I always did what I was told. I never rebelled. I would even say I was a people-pleaser.

Giving up on the miracle water was me being different from my usual self. I wanted to do something my elders did not want me to do. There was so much pent-up frustration that I was going against what my DNA dictated.

My family came around to see my point of view in a few days and agreed that we should stop this treatment. I returned to Hyderabad. It was time to work towards a kidney transplant.

In my journey with kidney disease, I had tried several alternate therapies. There is a pattern that I have recognized by now. A genuine well-wisher would come to know about a treatment. They would have heard about it from someone who claimed to know someone who benefited. They would call or send a message saying 'You have to try this.' I would get excited. I would meet the person who provided the solution. The nature of this person varied from a practitioner of the method to a businessman to a complete quack.

They would give me the medicines. Alongside was a chart of diet restrictions. They included a lot of false hopes. There were assurances that the treatment would cure me within a certain period of time. Many of them did not charge any money for their medicines. That gave the whole thing an aura of respectability.

'If they are not doing this for money, it has to be genuine,' was the refrain I always heard.

I have always believed in an undeniable, much stronger mental impact in a chronic disease like this. These alternate therapies messed with my mind repeatedly. There was so much hope to begin with. I subjected myself to severe diet restrictions besides the restrictions imposed by regular doctors. I bore everything. To what end? Nothing ever came out of it. Within a few weeks or months, I lost hope and eventually gave up, only to pick up another thread a little later.

One major problem I have with these people is that many of them have no basis for their assurances. It's as if they all want to try their therapies on me. If it works, great. If not, no harm done. My family and I treated these practitioners with a lot of respect, more than we did the conventional allopathic doctors. Most of these therapies and streams of treatment are beyond the purview of regulatory authorities. Anyone can make claims. Anyone can charge enormous sums of money. With little compunction, they hand out medicines that have not even undergone basic tests for safety.

I have yet to see for myself anyone being cured of kidney disease by any alternate therapy. I have seen many people being harmed by some of these therapies. This story is almost always the same. A shock diagnosis, fear of long-term dialysis and a realization that no permanent and workable cure exists precede a visit to an alternate therapy practitioner. After that, luck dictates whether you end up in the emergency ward of a hospital often leading to death or you go back to the nephrologist and agree to getting an access made after having resigned to dialysis as the best course of treatment.

If any alternate therapy worked, why would there be millions of people still undergoing dialysis? Conspiracy theorists claim that large dialysis organizations will not let cures for kidney failure come out and become mainstream. What else are we going to deny? Climate change? That the earth is a sphere?

Science demands proof. Let the proponents of these alternate therapies be subjected to the same rigour demanded of conventional therapy researchers. Let there be stringent regulations on all practitioners. Let no claims be allowed to be made without evidence and thorough clinical trials. That is the least the regulatory authorities can do to prevent the harm these quacks can cause.

Society also needs to change its mindset. Especially in India. There is a lot of suspicion towards practitioners of conventional medicine. The commercialization of medicine has a large role to play in strengthening this perception. Gone are the days when you went to your GP first for everything from a fever to cancer. They would treat most things. Then came the era of specialization. And then super specialization.

Today, a specialization exists for every little thing. GPs are almost extinct. Corporate hospitals rule the roost. No one wants to take a chance with their health. So, they end up trusting the largest hospital their money can afford. When things don't turn out the way they would like, they curse the medical system.

Non-conventional medicine, sometimes, may not be as commercial as conventional medicine. Well, you might end up paying a bomb to a random quack, but that amount is far less than what you would pay to get admitted to a corporate hospital in a metro city. That is why people are less hurt by such incidents than conventional medicine.

However, in emergencies, only conventional medicine has solutions. There are no Ayurvedic ICUs or homeopathic ventilators. People realize this and try not to cut the cord with their conventional medicine doctors. Though, in private conversations, they will always recommend this or that Ayurvedic or homeopathic or what-else-have-you doctor.

The government needs to step in and regulate alternate medicine. There is a Ministry of Ayurveda, Yoga & Naturopathy, Unani, Siddha and Homoeopathy (AYUSH). Only a few people know what they do about regulations. The government must formalize processes for clinical trials of these streams of medicine. Who knows? They might discover some effective drugs or therapies in the process.

* * *

3

A Flawed Solution

'What if I fall? Oh, but my darling, what if you fly!'

—J.M. Barrie

I soon got back into the routine of dialysis thrice a week. The old routine of going to Kamineni Hospital almost every other day resumed.

What was the next step?

We had allowed the kidney function to recover on its own, which hadn't happened, at least long term. We tried every alternate therapy that we could find. Nothing worked. What could we do next? I did not want to be on dialysis for the rest of my life.

The logical next step was a kidney transplant.[1]

The word 'transplant' had been bandied about at various points during the previous months. Someone would mention at the centre that one of the patients had got a transplant. I knew that it involved putting the donor's kidney into the patient's body. I did not know anything beyond that. It felt weird to have another person's organ in my body. But if it got me a regular life where I was not going to be chained to a machine, I was all right with it.

The first requirement, of course, was a donor. At that time, the cadaver transplant programme was non-existent in Hyderabad and most of India. We were not interested in getting a donor by paying money. Several such transplants happened during that period. We were against the idea.

So, we needed to figure out a donor from within the family. We ruled out my father because he was a chronic diabetic. My mother and brother were both very keen to donate a kidney. They would argue about who should donate. I was fortunate to have such an affectionate family where everyone was willing to give away one of their major organs so that I could lead a normal life. This was in sharp contrast to many families where donating a kidney would be discussed in hushed tones and family members did not want to donate their kidney. This is understandable because donating a major organ is a scary proposition. It would be a major surgery and most people are mortified of major surgeries.

I am not sure if it was the surgery that scared them or the fact that they would have to live with only one kidney. Science says that human beings can survive with one kidney. The lone kidney takes on the load of both kidneys and grows in size. Despite this, apprehensions remain and the number of live kidney donors is small.

There is also a huge gender disparity in India when it comes to kidney transplants. A 2019 study published in the *Indian Journal of Transplantation* by Dr Manisha Sahay of Osmania Medical College, Hyderabad, a nephrologist of repute, states:[2]

'Data from the National Organ Transplantation and Tissue Organization show that majority of living donations in India are from women and majority of organ recipients are men. Among organ transplant recipients, there are 23,682 men and a meagre 5,025 females.'

In India, women are always the ones who sacrifice. Most mothers donate to their children; wives to their husbands. The opposite rarely happens.

We went to meet Dr Sastry to discuss the possibility of a kidney transplant. He was very positive about the idea. When we asked him about who the donor should be, without the slightest hesitation he said that my mother would be the best choice as my brother was too young. Prasan was about eighteen years old then.

We started with tests. It was a very long process. A large number of tests were needed. From several blood tests to X-rays to HLA typing and a crossmatch. All the tests were on expected lines and nothing adverse came up. Both of us also had to undergo angiograms, which were also normal.

The entire process lasted a few months. After all the tests were done and everything was cleared, we decided on 11 November 1998 as the date of the transplant.

I was extremely anxious. Was this the beginning of a new dawn? Were all my troubles going to go away? Would I never need dialysis again? Were fluid restrictions going to become a thing of the past?

I was wary because of my past experience. Nothing had quite worked out before. The relief from steroids was temporary. The miracle water had no effect. Would the transplant work? When I read up online, there were mixed results even in patients who did not have aHUS. At the Kamineni centre itself, only a few weeks ago, a patient died shortly after the surgery because he did not recover from anaesthesia.

Among patients though, a transplant was the only possibility of redemption. So, when a transplant did not work out like in the case of the patient who died, we wondered, what was the way out? We would often talk to that man during his dialysis sessions. We were all happy that he was getting a transplant. And then all of a sudden, we got to know that he was no more. That left the other patients in the centre and me speechless.

In addition, I had the complication of my primary disease, aHUS.

Cyclosporin was the most commonly used immunosuppressant at the time of my kidney transplant. In my primary disease, aHUS, cyclosporin was suspected to cause recurrence of the disease in the transplanted kidney. Well, no one could say for sure but there were studies that found a link between cyclosporin and recurrent HUS. But there were also studies that showed that there was no link.

It was very important to take the right decision regarding which immunosuppressant to use. I did a lot of research on the Internet, took printouts of all the articles and gave them to Dr Sastry.

After a few days, I went to him with my parents to discuss the subject. He asked me what I thought we should be using. I was a little surprised. When your doctor wants to know what you think about such an important decision, it could mean that he wants to involve you in this process. It could also mean something else. That he is not sure. And that can be disconcerting.

You could not fault Dr Sastry for that, though. There was a lot of evidence to support both decisions. While there were cases where cyclosporin had been used and had caused recurrence of HUS, there were several studies which reported no recurrence despite the use of cyclosporin. What do you do when you have inconclusive data?

We discussed this and Dr Sastry felt we should use cyclosporin. It was because this was something nephrologists had experience using. Most of their kidney transplant patients were on this drug. When there is no clear evidence to support not using a drug, might as well go with it because it is something you're used to.

Not having any evidence to suggest the contrary, I was on board with the decision. I had no medical knowledge, not even an MBBS degree. All I had to go by were articles on the Internet. And those articles, too, were divided. There was not a single piece of information or guideline that recommended or advised against the use of cyclosporin in kidney transplants.

This was akin to taking a path to get to your destination, not knowing whether the path led to where you wanted to go or not. You have a feeling it might. But then again, it might not. In the absence of a clear map, you have no choice.

Amidst these circumstances, I started preparing myself mentally for a kidney transplant. It could be the beginning of a new life. If the transplant succeeded, I could get on with my life. Not needing to connect to a dialysis machine itself would be a relief. I might also be able to go to the US for my master's. I could lead a normal life.

Normality. What an underrated thing! Most people don't want a normal life. They want a special life. Normal people are often considered weak. They are called losers.

For dialysis patients, normality is utopia. Give me a normal life. That's all I crave. A life where I don't need to rely on a machine to live. In which I don't need to stay away from something as basic as water. Where I can eat as much fruit as I want to. Are these really too much to ask for?

With this promise of unshackled freedom, I went in for the most important surgery of my life.

* * *

My mother and I got admitted to Kamineni Hospital on 10 November, a day before the surgery. It was getting a little cold in Hyderabad. I preferred the cold over the hot summers the city experienced. It never got biting cold, though. It was just enough to be called winter. We were in adjacent rooms.

I had dialysis that day. It could be the last time I would undergo the pain of the two thick needles in my left arm. They took me back to my room once I completed the dialysis session.

Dr Dakshinamurthy came over that evening and discussed the plan. He thought I would have a sleepless night and gave me a sedative. He was sure that despite the sedative, I would not sleep in anticipation of the transplant the next day. I slept as if it was a normal day, though.

After sixteen months of uncertainty, the morning of the transplant came. The day of liberation. When all my troubles would end. The enormity of the day started to grow on me. My heart was racing.

The hospital's team came with a wheelchair, and I sat on it. We went to the operation theatre (OT) area. This area had several OTs where surgeries could simultaneously be conducted. The chief surgeon, Dr Rama Raju, came and greeted me. He was the chief urologist at Kamineni Hospital. He and his team would work on me. Dr Revathi, who was Dr Rama Raju's wife, was also a surgeon and would work on my mother. They also took my signatures on several consent forms.

Soon, the OT team transferred me to the operation theatre. It had one central area, where there was a raised metallic platform with a thin rexine-like material. They asked me to lie on it. It was at a height that made it easy for the surgeon and their team to work. A lever could adjust the height. There were several slots to attach fittings to enable placement of the patient's hands or legs in varied positions. That allowed the operating team to access and work on the relevant body part. There was a large fitting right above, which had several lights that they could turn on in any direction and at any height, to focus on the patient's body part that was being operated upon. They set the air conditioners of the OT at quite low temperatures.

The teams began their work. It was going to be a long day.

One nurse from Dr Rama Raju's team put an intravenous line in my right hand that would be used to administer any drugs during the surgery. She also placed a mask on my nose and mouth and asked me to breathe. Dr Rama Raju began asking me trivial questions such as which places I had travelled to within India. Within a few seconds, even as I began recounting the locations, I lost consciousness. I had no awareness or recollection of what happened from then on.

Dr Rama Raju cleansed the skin over my stomach with disinfectant.

He scrubbed several hundred millilitres of povidone-iodine solution on my stomach to make sure that the area was germ-free. He then made a deep incision in the right side of my stomach to gain access to the inner part of my abdomen.

In the adjoining operation theatre, Dr Revathi and her team worked on my mother. They administered general anaesthesia to her as well. Dr Revathi operated on my mother and removed her left kidney. The vessels that served as input and output to the kidney were closed. They transferred the extracted kidney to the OT where I was being worked on.

Dr Rama Raju placed the kidney inside my body and connected the various circulatory systems in my body to make sure that blood flowed to the kidney and it passed the urine produced to my bladder. The new kidney started functioning immediately. It began producing urine and started sending it to the bladder.

Contrary to general belief, the two native kidneys stay in the body. So, after the surgery, I had three kidneys in my body.

Dr Revathi stitched up the opening she had made to remove my mother's kidney. Dr Rama Raju closed my stomach.

They placed a collecting tube in each of us that collected and drained all the excess blood that would 'leak' so that it did not cause any complications. They also placed a catheter inside me to collect all the urine the transplanted kidney was producing.

When the surgery was complete, they moved me to a transplant care unit to help me recover from the anaesthesia. After a while, the doctors got worried since I was not recovering from anaesthesia. There was panic all round, and they summoned the anaesthetist. They tried a cocktail of drugs to get me out of my peaceful slumber. Since that might have caused cardiac issues, they called a senior cardiologist and a group of other specialists as well. They connected me to a ventilator.

All this commotion terrified my family. Everyone started praying hard.

While my mother had no clue what was happening, the situation petrified my father. It scared the rest of the family as well. What was happening? All they saw was doctors rushing in and out. Would someone tell them what was going on?

Within an hour, because of the efforts of the doctors, I came out of my stupor. I was stable. All this time, I was unconscious. I had no clue about the entire drama that had just occurred.

When I came to, I felt a soreness in my throat and was coughing a little. I found myself in the transplant care unit, lying on a bed. A nurse was there in the room. I was dying to know what had happened during the surgery.

'Sister, how did the transplant go?'

'It went very well. You are fine!'

'Nice!' I thought to myself. I asked her about the soreness in my throat. She said that was okay, and it was because of the ventilator. She was silent about the happenings of the last twenty-four hours. I assumed that they used the ventilator as a routine part of the transplant surgery. I had no clue that it was used while they revived me from deep anaesthesia.

They put me on intravenous (IV) fluids, and I was peeing gallons through a catheter by then. My new kidney was working.

For the next few days, the routine continued. They would draw blood every morning for tests, and the nephrologist and the surgeon would visit and check on me. I was started a liquid diet, then moved to semi-solid food and then, solids. I had a steady stream of visitors who could see me through a sealed, transparent glass window. They would communicate using sign language.

After about nine days of the transplant, they moved me to a private room.

* * *

On the eleventh day after the transplant, Dr Dakshinamurthy came to my room in the morning.

'Your creatinine is a little high. I have asked for a repeat test.'

My heart started beating fast. This should not have happened. Maybe a mistake. Let's wait for the repeat test. A few hours later, I learned that the repeat test showed the same value. Now what?

The doctors returned after a while. The decision was to give me a massive dose of steroids to force the kidney to behave and get a biopsy to find out what was happening. They took me to a room next to the dialysis centre and administered a large dose of the steroid prednisolone. The same day, they performed a biopsy. This biopsy was much simpler than the earlier ones, as they had to draw tissue from the new kidney that was right under the skin of the stomach.

The creatinine rose the next day as well. Again, prednisolone.

The third day as well, creatinine levels went up. Again, prednisolone.

No change.

By the twentieth day post the transplant, my creatinine almost touched ten. I had to get dialysis. This was a big setback. I felt like I was being sent back to jail after being released for a crime I never committed. 'Why dialysis?' my family asked.

Dr Sastry came to see me the next day. He told me that they were thinking about what to do, but there were no simple answers. He asked my parents to arrange for another immunosuppressant called mycophenolate mofetil (MMF). They might have to switch to that from cyclosporin. It was not available in Hyderabad, and we would have had to get in touch with a distributor to arrange for it. My parents found a distributor and the new capsules were there in about three or four days.

After a few more days, the biopsy report came in. Dr Sastry came to my room and said HUS had recurred. He asked me not to worry and that they would figure out a plan. Stepping outside the room, he walked up to the nursing station and took my file in his hands. He spent a good twenty minutes going over the pages; looking out of the window; thinking, and looking at the pages again. In the end, he wrote in all capitals, 'STOP CYCLOSPORIN'. He started me on MMF.

I had to get continuous dialysis. I felt like this setback had destroyed my soul. While I was going for dialysis, coming back, eating food, watching TV, sleeping and doing all that, from the inside, I was numb, devoid of any feelings.

This broke my family as well. Both my grandmothers cried when they got to know.

I was started on MMF. They also sent pictures of my biopsy slides to different doctors and specialists in India and the US through email. Nothing useful emerged. MMF too wasn't acting. But Dr Sastry said we needed to wait for a few days. After a few days, he asked for a few more days. I could see the initial phase of my disease recurring as well. It was always one more week. One more week. One more week.

Except, the weeks never ended.

After about a month of the transplant, during a dialysis session, Dr Sastry came to my bed and said, 'We must give up now.'

That was the verdict. It did not come as a great surprise to me. But that was the end. Officially.

For several days after the transplant, I thought a lot about what had happened.

How did I get this disease? What had happened in the last eighteen months had shaken my entire life. Instead of happily pursuing my master's in the US, here I was on a hospital bed being wheeled in and out of dialysis.

Was it because of the vaccines? Many others took them. Was it because of the antibiotics and painkillers I had taken a month before I got this? Nothing that dozens of others hadn't taken in the past.

I had a disease called Idiopathic Thrombocytopenia Purpura (ITP) in my childhood, which they treated successfully with steroids. This disease also had similar symptoms as aHUS. Could it have had a link to the current disease? Was that episode actually an aHUS flare? At that time, no one knew much about aHUS. Doctors probably associated it with a disease that closely matched the symptoms. The word idiopathic means 'of unknown cause'.

A kidney transplant was to be the redemption I needed. It was going to be the end of the struggle and freedom from dialysis. What happened then? Why did my disease recur? Was cyclosporin the right decision? Had the kidney transplant been doomed from the start? Who could tell? We knew so little about the disease that we couldn't say with any certainty how the transplant would have turned out with another immunosuppressant.

Those were the days when there was no facility to measure cyclosporin levels. It came much later. This is now an important part of post-transplant care. Was the dose of cyclosporin higher than what I had needed? When I showed the slides from the biopsy of the transplanted kidney to a nephro-pathologist I knew, she said it could have been cyclosporin toxicity as well. But she could not say for sure.

All these questions remained unanswered for years.

Since then, researchers have made a lot of progress on this disease. We now know that we shouldn't even have attempted the kidney transplant. Based on the scientific evidence available at the time of writing this book, the transplant was doomed to fail. Recurrence was a high possibility.

Several years later, I sent my blood samples to a lab in the UK. Prof. Tim Goodship, a leading researcher in aHUS, led the lab. They found that I had a genetic mutation[3] in my body, which was implicated in this disease. With that mutation, the chance of recurrence was over 95 per cent.

Back in 1998, however, doctors did not know any of this. So, we cannot blame the doctors. We now know that my genes were responsible for the recurrence.[4]

Over the years, researchers have identified several such mutations. They have also identified several 'triggers' for the disease and recurrence after a kidney transplant. Back in 1998, however, the doctors did not know all this. We were fighting a battle blindfolded where we did not know who our enemies were. Not knowing what weapons they had, we were waving our swords in the air. It was a fight we were bound to lose.

* * *

4

Some Peace at Last

'Some of you say, "Joy is greater than sorrow," and others say,
"Nay, sorrow is the greater."
But I say unto you, they are inseparable.
Together they come, and when one sits alone with you
at your board, remember that the other is asleep upon your bed.'
—Kahlil Gibran

I was back to regular, thrice a week haemodialysis sessions at Kamineni Hospital. About a month later, I began having a mild fever. This happened every evening. It was not too high to panic but not too low to ignore. I brought this up with Dr Sastry. He sounded a little anxious. An ultrasound scan showed that the transplanted kidney had grown in size and was scarred. We would need to remove it.

So, I underwent another major surgery where they put me under general anaesthesia again and removed the kidney. I was told later that the kidney was in such terrible shape that while removing it, it broke. Dr Sastry added that I was lucky that we had removed it in time. Else, we would have had an emergency.

I started researching about kidney disease on the Internet again around that time. It was early 1999. I stumbled upon a term called peritoneal dialysis (PD). This was a modality where dialysis happens without any external machine. You simply insert some fluid into your stomach through a catheter and dialysis happens across a membrane called the peritoneum.[1]

To me, this is just one example of the wonders of nature. Who would have imagined that this obscure membrane could be suitable for dialysis? They may not be as efficient as the kidneys, but then their primary purpose was not cleaning blood. How did evolution make these membranes capable of clearing out toxins and excess fluid? How did scientists discover the magic that these membranes could perform?[2]

To be able to do this, a minor surgery[3] needs to be performed which allows the patient to have an 'exchange'. The process of removal of the old fluid and infusion of fresh fluid is called an 'exchange'.

What I read online sounded quite promising. Diet and fluid restrictions were minimal. I could do it at home. Many people could lead quite a normal life with it. I was wondering if the modality was available in India at all. No one had told me about it. I had seen no patients who were on PD.

At that time, PD was very rare in India and most of the world. Less than 5 per cent of patients who were on dialysis underwent PD. But I had decided that I wanted to try it. Two things attracted me to this modality. One was that there would be less diet and fluid restrictions. The second was that I did not have to go to the hospital thrice a week.

I decided to ask Dr Sastry about it. I was sure he would say no and that would be the end. So, one morning, when Dr Sastry came to my bedside while I was on dialysis in Kamineni Hospital and carried out the usual examination, I asked him if I could try PD. 'Sure', he said. Well, that was easy, I thought.

I was not sure if things would materialize. I was used to things not panning out the way I wanted. If PD sounded too good to be true, it would never materialize for me. Some problem would crop up. It could be a clinical reason or a logistical reason. Maybe they wouldn't operate in Hyderabad. Maybe it would not suit my body. I was very sure it would not happen.

The events of the past two years had messed up my mind. The confident twenty-one-year-old, who had won gold medals at school and college and was ready to conquer the world, had metamorphosed into a pessimistic twenty-three-year-old who believed that everything that could go wrong, would. After having my US dreams crushed, this disease did not even allow me the respite that most young kidney patients get—that of a kidney transplant. I had become used to setbacks by then.

To my surprise, in the very next session itself, Dr Dakshinamurthy came to me and said that he had arranged for the clinical coordinator from the PD company to come and meet me so that we could plan to start PD. I started getting excited. Things looked like they were moving.

The clinical coordinator from Baxter, Venkataramana, came a few days later and explained the entire process. I had also continued my reading on the subject on the Internet.

There would be a minor surgery where they would insert the PD catheter somewhere in my stomach and then, they would train me for a few days at the hospital. Once I got the hang of it, I could go home and do it on my own. The surgery usually left a scar on the stomach. But in those days, laparoscopy was increasingly being used to do the PD catheter insertion, which caused only a small, buttonhole-sized scar. An experienced surgeon from

Australia was going to be visiting the hospital in a few days for the kidney transplant of a young girl. They had arranged for him to do my PD catheter surgery too.

The day of the surgery came and proceeded without too much of a fuss. The catheter was in place. A day after the surgery, I had an intense, sharp stinging pain in my lower abdomen. They said that the tip of the catheter was touching the nerve ends in my peritoneal cavity. The pain would go once fluid was infused. But that could not be done until the surgery wound healed.

A few days passed. It was time for infusion of fluid for the first time. All this while, I was on continued haemodialysis. I was on fluid and diet restrictions. I was waiting for PD to start so that I did not have to bother about restrictions. They started with one litre of fluid. I could feel a cool liquid filling within me. It was a rather strange sensation.

After a couple of hours, they removed the fluid. It was yellow, like normal urine. This was expected since it was replicating kidney function. Fresh fluid was infused once the old fluid had drained out.

Over the next few days, they gradually increased the volume of fluid until I was doing two litres in every exchange. There was a minor discomfort in my stomach due to the fluid in it. I would feel relieved when the fluid drained. But I did not mind it at all. I did not have any diet and fluid restrictions, and I was enjoying the freedom.

Fluid restrictions have a disproportionate impact on the psyche of dialysis patients. One young patient I knew once told me that he had instructed his mother to give him one full glass each of water, buttermilk, coffee and coconut water respectively when he was about to die. Most dialysis patients cannot even think of having something as simple as a full glass of water. So, when I could suddenly do that on peritoneal dialysis, I was exhilarated. I felt like I was being freed from chains tied to my feet that prevented me from moving.

* * *

I went back home from hospital and got into a routine. Four exchanges every day—the first when I woke up every morning, the second before or after lunch, the third around 5 p.m. and the last before sleeping.

I had to be very careful about infections. The chances of infection at the point where the catheter goes in—called the exit site—are very high.

I had to wash my hands thoroughly before every exchange. Every morning, after a shower, I had to clean the exit site with a disinfectant solution and then cover it with gauze and tape it securely.

Within a few months, I had become quite comfortable with PD. I put on weight, most of it because of all the glucose that was being absorbed by my body from the dialysis solution. That didn't bother me at all. I relished the freedom this modality offered me. I was eating and drinking all I wanted. Diet and fluid restrictions were a thing of the past.

I soon took up a job as I was feeling wasted and needed to get some activity for my brain. For the first time in my life, after being diagnosed with kidney disease, I felt like doing something. I started feeling almost normal, as I could think of things other than my health. Feeling like a bird freed from a cage, I needed to fend for myself now.

My energy levels increased. This normality was not something my body and mind were used to since the past year-and-a-half. I relished the feeling. It was almost akin to a new birth.

While I was looking for work, I learnt that my mother's friend Hemanti and her husband Vijay were running a software company called Suma Computers. They were doing some interesting projects for the United Nations. My mother asked Hemanti aunty if I could come and work there for a few hours every day. She agreed and was thrilled that I was trying to get back to a normal life.

I started going to their office in the morning and returned home in time for my afternoon exchange. After lunch, I would work from home. This routine brought a dramatic change in my mental outlook. For the first time since my diagnosis in July 1997, I was doing something productive.

I was enjoying my work. I was learning Visual Basic, a software development language, from the team at Suma Computers, and contributing to the projects being executed.

That year, I went for a vacation to Kodaikanal, a hill station in south India. This would not have been possible if I had been on haemodialysis because the nearest dialysis centre was a four-hour drive away. One other thing that made vacations on PD possible was that Baxter, the company that manufactured and distributed the PD fluid that I used, had an excellent network. You could go to any place and you were likely to find a supplier of dialysis fluid close enough.

This was a big change from the dreary days on haemodialysis. It was almost impossible to go on a holiday away from home. I had to find a dialysis centre close enough. I had to schedule sessions there. And, I could never be sure of the quality of the centre. What kinds of technicians ran the centre? Did they follow proper protocols?

With PD, holidays were a breeze. All I needed to do was to call the Baxter team and get the contact details of a distributor of bags who was close to the destination. Call them a little in advance to book the bags and then pick them up on the designated date. Simple!

I got a huge break, work-wise, later that year. Obul Kambham, a friend of my uncle, Paul, came to Hyderabad from the US. He was about to start a software development company focusing on the Apple platform. He met me and asked me to join him as co-founder. I was excited. I spoke to Hemanti aunty and explained the situation. She let me pursue this opportunity, as it would allow me to grow even further.

Obul introduced me to the wonderful world of Apple. I started learning WebObjects, a development platform for web-based applications using Apple technologies. Obul roped in a few more people and we registered a company called Grey Matter Software Pvt. Ltd. We later changed the name of the company to Effigent, derived by juxtaposing efficient and intelligent.

After taking up an office space in Secunderabad, we hired a bunch of developers and started teaching everyone WebObjects. Work started coming in as well.

Things couldn't have been better. My work was excellent. I had no diet and fluid restrictions. There were no needles being jabbed into my arms every other day. The two exchanges during the day were a problem. The ones to be done during the morning and night were not a problem. It was only the middle two exchanges.

I discussed this with Dr Sastry, who suggested that I could consider a cycler. The way a cycler works is that you hook up to a machine at night and it performs the exchanges automatically with shorter dwell periods. That way, you do not have to do anything during the day.

The only problem was that the machine was not portable, so you needed to do manual exchanges during the day when you went out of town or were away from home.

I underwent a test which told us if I was suited to the cycler. The answer was vague,[4] but we went ahead anyway.

We went on another vacation in the subsequent year. This time, it was in Mahabaleshwar, a hill station in western India. I did manual exchanges during this trip.

I was now leading an almost normal life, apart from the
exchanges at night on the cycler and the morning, post shower
dressing of the exit site. Of course, if I lifted my shirt to expose
my stomach, you would see this cloth pouch tied around my
stomach with a plastic tube in it.

A few months later, I switched back to my original doctor,
Dr Girish Narayen.

In April 2004, I had finished five years of PD and things
were going very well. Baxter even featured me in the 'PD Heroes'
section of their quarterly newsletter.

I was thrilled that life had gotten back to normal after all
the turbulence of the past few years. No one could tell I was on
dialysis by looking at me, if they did not know my history. I was
leading a normal life. I was working full-time, playing table tennis,
travelling once in a while and, what was very important to me
then, I had no diet and fluid restrictions.

PD showed me the power of being proactive in life with
kidney disease. If I hadn't looked up the Internet for more
information, chances are that I would never have learnt about
PD. Once I found out about it, I spoke to my nephrologist about
it and asked him if I could do it. Only because I did that, did PD
happen.

Two problems of Indian healthcare come to the fore. Why
were all options not presented to me at the beginning? Why was
the decision to do haemodialysis taken for me? Why was I not
even told about PD?

Making the patient a part of the decision-making process
cannot be an afterthought. It cannot be a low-priority activity.
Indian healthcare is constrained by the workforce. There are very
few doctors for an enormous population. Agreed. I still don't
think that is a valid excuse for not discussing all options with
patients. It's their life and they deserve to know what options they
have.

One explanation for this is that Indian patients don't want to take any responsibility of care into their hands. They would much rather that the healthcare staff did everything. PD is largely done independently by patients themselves. The outcomes are broadly in the hands of the patients themselves. Many patients dislike the enormity of this burden. It is possible that Indian nephrologists have got used to patients refusing PD because they don't want to do things on their own. Over time, they may have stopped offering that option altogether.

The other problem is that patients are rarely proactive. Very few patients attempt to find out more about the disease. They don't bother to read up online about the latest treatment options and on what's good and bad about each option. They are content with the doctors' advice and follow it blindly. This has been changing with the proliferation of the Internet, especially mobile phone-based Internet. These days, more and more people are trying to find out about their disease and treatment options.

For me, not being proactive was not an option. It was simple. If I did not find out what was good for me, no one else would. Busy doctors rarely had time for individualistic care. I had to fend for myself. The dividends were huge. For the first time in several months, I felt more in control of my life. I did not feel helpless. The ability to work, to travel and have fun, brought with it a dramatic difference in my mindset. I did not feel 'sick' any more.

* * *

5

To Hell and Back

'We do, then, deserve to be punished
beyond all expectations.
Hell hath no fury like a woman scorned.
Mother Nature is grieving, you have been warned.'

—Dan Brown

It was nearing the end of 2004, a time when there wasn't much work happening in office because most of our clients in the US were off for their annual Christmas break. A few colleagues and I wanted to go somewhere for a few days and take a holiday.

We had not planned ahead, and because of that, we had to rule out many places like Goa. Travel bookings were difficult. Accommodation was even more difficult.

An uncle in Chennai got us two cottages at a resort in Mahabalipuram, a coastal town close to Chennai in south India for the nights of 25, 26 and 27 December.

So, four of my colleagues from Effigent and I set out and reached Chennai late in the evening. We took a taxi and headed towards Mahabalipuram. We took the picturesque New Mahabalipuram Road, which ran parallel to the east coast of the country. Even in the night, the sea was beautiful. As we left the hullabaloo of the city and the sky became clearer, the light from the moon reflected on the sea waves breaking against the shore along which our car traversed. We stopped for a few minutes to take in this spectacle of nature.

The powerful waves, the pollution-free atmosphere and the glorious weather got all our spirits up and we were looking forward to having a great time.

We reached at around 9 p.m. We checked-in into our cottages. To our delight, they gave us rooms right on the beach. There was sand under our feet as we stepped out of our rooms. We freshened up and went to the open-air restaurant. We finished dinner and then went to relax at the beach.

There was a row of reclining chairs on the beach facing the sea. We sat there, enjoying the breeze for about an hour and planned what we would do the next day. We decided to go back to the beach the next morning, spend time there and then, go over to Mahabalipuram city and do some sightseeing. I had learnt about the Shore Temple and the five *rathas* in school in history class. Both were architectural marvels that had been built centuries ago but were still intact. I was looking forward to seeing them.

We then went over to play table tennis for a while. It was around 2.30 a.m. We were all quite tired by then. We decided that we had all had enough for the day and went back to our cottages and fell asleep in minutes.

About four hours hence, unbeknownst to us, several thousand kilometres away, off the west coast of Sumatra in Indonesia, deep under the sea, an earthquake struck. It was the third most severe ever. Recording over nine on the Richter scale, it unleashed a force that was 1500 times that of the atom bomb that devastated Hiroshima. The earthquake caused an 800-mile-long gash in the earth's surface below the ocean. This caused the displacement of a massive amount of water, which started moving at a huge velocity with frightening force. It was like a gigantic wall of water rushing towards land.

Within thirty minutes, a tsunami had struck the northern tip of Indonesia, destroying the coast and killing thousands of people in seconds. It rendered more than half a million people homeless. Another tsunami hit the Andaman and Nicobar Islands next, killing several hundred. Several such devastating tsunamis hit Bangladesh, Burma and Thailand, destroying their coastlands.

Around two hours after the first quake, another earthquake was recorded near the Andaman and Nicobar Islands. This was 7.3 on the Richter scale. A tsunami was now headed towards Sri Lanka and India.

We were all sleeping and dreaming about the next day, unaware of what lay in store for us over the next few hours.

* * *

When we woke in the morning and stepped out of our cottages, a gentle breeze greeted us. We took turns to lie on the hammock outside our cottage and chatted for a while. We then ordered breakfast and started getting ready, planning to sit at the beach for some time and then head out to see the monuments.

I ordered a plate of idlis for myself, finished my peritoneal dialysis exchange and was watching TV. My roommate, Pushkar, went to take a shower.

Suddenly, I noticed water coming into the room from under the door. I did not know what to make of it. I shouted out to Pushkar. The first gush was about a centimetre deep. The water went back as fast as it came in, only to be followed by repeated gushes, each bigger than the earlier.

By then, Pushkar had come out, wrapped in a towel, wondering what was happening.

Thoughts crossed my confused mind, trying to make sense of the situation. I had heard that the day prior had been a full moon day and I was wondering if the tide was a little stronger than usual due to that. That would have explained the water coming in this far. I wondered why no one at the resort had warned us about it. I also thought that this might have been a regular occurrence and the resort management had been stupid for not telling us.

A huge gush of water opened the door, which flooded the entire room. Within moments, we were neck-deep in water. The next instant, water was sucked out, closing the door with it. This pattern repeated several times over, making it difficult for us to get out of the cottage. A strong gush of water came inward, pushing us inside with it. It was followed by a potent force from outside that appeared to be sucking the water out of the room, closing the door behind it. We were stuck.

During one such cycle, Pushkar kept the door open and what he saw petrified him. An enormous wall of water, hundreds of feet high, was hurtling towards us.

He held on to the pavement above the window of the cottage and somehow pulled himself out of the room. He shouted out to me to follow him. I trudged towards the door. It was quite difficult. The inward gush of water forced me backwards. The outward gush took me towards the door but shut it. I glanced to my side and noticed the television set, refrigerator and cots bobbing up and down in the water.

Was this it, I wondered? The last way I wanted to die was by drowning. Random thoughts crossed my mind. The risk of infection of my exit site, the dirty water I had ingested, everything was scary.

The next time the water came in, the door opened and before it could close with the outward gush, I put my left leg in between to prevent the door from closing. I did not want to drown and die. This primordial urge to live gave me the strength to force myself through the doorway. I got out of the room. Pushkar and one of the other guys held my hands and pulled me out. We made our way to a higher piece of land inside the resort and caught our breath. Within a few minutes, my other colleagues joined us.

None of us spoke a single word for the next several minutes. The water receded. My colleagues wanted to go back to the room to salvage what was left. I refused to join them.

All this while, we thought that this was something very local, confined to the resort or, at the most, to a kilometre around where we were. We had no inkling that this was one of the worst natural disasters to have hit humanity.

The resort staff was in total disarray. People were shocked. No one knew what had happened. We went to the resort owner's cottage and kept our stuff on the first floor. Then, we went and sat on the terrace, unsure of what would happen next.

After a while, Pushkar and a couple of others went down to assess the situation and decide on what to do next. Our taxi driver had parked the car on a road that was at a height, and the water had not reached that part. The car was safe and untouched by the water. We decided we would go to the car and head back to Chennai.

In the meantime, we learned similar incidents had happened in Chennai and other coastal cities, too.

We went down, took our stuff and walked towards the exit of the resort. To do this, we had to wade across a large pool of water that had collected between the road and our side of the resort.

We got into the car and started towards Chennai. The locals advised us to take the old Mahabalipuram road since parts of the new one had been inundated.

Along the way, we saw many people running helter-skelter. There was panic and grief everywhere. It was as if something horrible had happened, but people did not know what it was and what to make of it.

We reached the city of Chennai in a few hours. On the way, we called our folks at home and told them we were safe. We drove straight to Apollo Hospital, where there were no signs of anyone knowing what had just happened. A couple of my relatives came there. We got first aid at the casualty ward and then went to their house. There, during the day, through television news reports, I came to know about the enormity of the damage that the tsunami had caused in so many places. It had killed several thousand. Several million were now homeless. We were lucky to have survived, as this was one of the worst tsunamis to hit humankind in recorded history.

I took the evening flight to Hyderabad, a day after I started out amidst the most eventful twenty-four hours of my life.

* * *

Once I reached Hyderabad, over the next week, I got back to my routine after getting over the traumatic time I had at Mahabalipuram.

One thing that was bothering me was that my catheter and exit site had been soaked in the filthy water that the tsunami brought with it. The doctors always advised me to take care of it like a mother would take care of her newborn. This was the most brutal assault possible on my exit site.

I went over to Dr Girish Narayen and discussed the entire episode with him. He prescribed a strong antibiotic for a few days as a precaution, which I took. Everything seemed to be all right.

A few months after this incident, one morning, while cleaning my exit site, I noticed a little pus around it. My exit site was infected.

I called the Baxter clinical coordinator, Venkataramana. He came over and examined the exit site. I went over to Dr Girish

Narayen. He put me on antibiotics and asked me to dress the exit
site twice on a daily basis. We also sent the pus for a culture.

Dr Girish Narayen suggested that I get a fistula made in case
we needed to do haemodialysis at some point. That seemed like
an overkill. Why would I ever need to go back to haemodialysis?
This was a minor infection and we could take care of it. But I went
with Dr Narayen's advice.

I went to meet Dr P.C. Gupta, an excellent vascular surgeon in
Hyderabad, to discuss the fistula. Dr Gupta was the best vascular
surgeon in the city and among the best in the country. He had
done his MBBS from the Armed Forces Medical College, Pune,
and then pursued a post-graduation from PGI, Chandigarh.
In 1997, he completed a fellowship in vascular surgery from
Nagoya, Japan. He had gained an excellent reputation in his
field and was the first choice for anyone looking for a vascular
surgeon in Hyderabad. He was young, but what was heartening
to know was that his early success had not taken away his
humility. Approachable and good-natured, he had everything
you looked for in a doctor.

We set a date. They wheeled me into the OT for a surgery
that was expected to take about an hour at most. I was awake
during the surgery. Dr Gupta and his assistant surgeon were
working on the fistula on my upper left arm. I was following
their conversation and after about an hour, it seemed as if they
were about to wind up. However, at one point, the conversation
became a little worried, and they sounded a little perplexed.

Dr Gupta said, 'Mr Shah, there is a slight problem. The vein
seems to be blocked and we're not getting a good flow. We will
need to connect this to another vein and this may take some more
time.' There was nothing more I could say apart from, 'Okay,
doctor.'

What was to take one hour took about three and a half
hours. My family outside the OT were panicking. What was

going on? Dr Gupta briefed them only after the surgery. The surgery concluded with a functioning fistula.

In the meantime, the exit site pus culture identified the bacteria as pseudomonas aeruginosa.

I had attended a medical conference on peritoneal dialysis about a year ago, sponsored by Baxter. Only doctors and technicians attended such conferences. But I knew one of the senior executives at Baxter, Harish Natarajan. Harish's mother was the neighbour of my sister-in-law's mother. He often visited Hyderabad to see his mom, and my sister-in-law introduced me to him. Harish was an alumnus of the reputed Indian Institute of Management Ahmedabad (IIMA). When I got in touch with him, he headed Baxter's Renal Division in India and then, the Philippines.

My proactive approach towards my health impressed Harish, and we continued to be in touch. He invited me to the PD conference to learn more about what was new in the PD world. I had attended a session on infections and I remember the speaker mentioning that infections caused by the pseudomonas family of bacteria were hard to eradicate.

The exit site infection seemed to settle within a few days, but that was not the last I had heard from the deadly pseudomonas.

A few weeks later, I developed a tunnel infection. The tunnel is the path that the PD catheter takes from outside, below the skin, to the peritoneum. A portion of my skin above the tunnel had become red and swollen. These were sure signs of an infection. I had to take oral antibiotics again, and it looked like the infection had gone.

The doctors then decided to reposition the catheter because of the recurrent nature of the pseudomonas bacteria. So, I underwent a surgery where they repositioned the catheter. The peritoneal end of the catheter was in the peritoneum itself.

They repositioned only the outer end of the catheter to take another path.

Within a few weeks, the tunnel infection recurred. The pseudomonas devils were not giving up just as yet.

At that point, they decided to remove the PD catheter; give the entire area some rest, let the infections heal and then put in a new catheter. I would need to go back on haemodialysis for a while, after all. Dr Girish Narayen's experience had helped.

So, I was back on the operating table, where they removed the PD catheter. And, I was also back—after over six years—to what I hated the most in life. Haemodialysis. Back to the needle jabs; back to the diet and fluid restrictions. But I took solace in the fact that this was a temporary phase and I would be back on PD soon.

I switched to a hospital called Krishna Institute of Medical Sciences (KIMS) which was closer to where I lived. It was much more convenient.

We waited for a couple of months and then planned the re-insertion of the new PD catheter. This meant yet another surgery. The surgery went well, but on the way back home from the hospital, I had the most unbearable pain. Usually, painkillers are administered immediately after surgery and once the effect wears off, there is pain, but it is fairly well-controlled by oral painkillers. But this time, the pain was so bad, I was crying. Once we reached home, I took some powerful painkillers, and the pain reduced.

So, I was now back on PD. I started manual exchanges. However, the efficiency of the dialysis had reduced. The amount of water that was being removed was much less than required. While this was being investigated, I had to do a few sessions of haemodialysis so that I got good clearance. So, I was doing both haemodialysis and PD for a while.

This was a complex problem. We did not know how to handle it. Why had the efficacy of the dialysis reduced? The doctors thought it could be because of the adhesions that had formed in the peritoneal cavity after the large number of surgeries I had had. They were not sure if they could do anything about it and continued my haemodialysis for a while until we got clarity. I was continuing my PD as well.

While continuing to stay updated on my disease and developments in the space, I had often come across the name of a Dr Georgi Abraham on the Internet in connection with PD. He seemed to be an expert in PD and had written several research papers on PD in India. I went to Chennai to consult with him on this.

'We're here to meet Dr Georgi Abraham.'

'Doctor has not yet come, sir. Please wait. You're sixth on the list.'

'Sixth!' I thought to myself. After he came, it would be a good one hour, at least, before we got to meet him. My dad and I settled down in the waiting area on one of the upper floors of the Madras Medical Mission Hospital (Triple M Hospital) at Mogappair in Chennai. Dr Georgi Abraham primarily practised there.

Having graduated from TD Medical College in Alleppey in Kerala, he then did an MD in general medicine from Mysore University. After that, he completed FRCP (London) and FRCP (Glasgow). He is widely regarded as the father of peritoneal dialysis in India, as he was the one who started PD in India and did a lot of research in this area.

Dr Abraham seemed to be a very affable person, with genuine concern for his patients. He analysed all the evidence and then suggested that we try 'Extraneal' solution instead of the regular 'Dianeal' solution. Extraneal solution was another type of PD solution that was composed of a chemical called icodextrin at a concentration of 7.5 per cent and had some properties that were better than Dianeal, which was dextrose. Dianeal was available in multiple strengths such as 1.5 per cent, 2.5 per cent and 4.25 per cent whereas Extraneal was only available in the

7.5 per cent variant. Extraneal did not cause any weight gain and was also more suitable for a night dwell where a sizeable amount of fluid could be pulled off. Dr Abraham thought we might get better fluid removal with this solution.

Extraneal was not yet being used widely in India. But I got a few bags through Harish Natarajan of Baxter. I tried the Extraneal solution, but it did not make any difference to the clearance either. I still could not get enough dialysis.

We went back to discuss this with Dr Georgi Abraham.

* * *

As we waited for Dr Georgi to arrive and pass his verdict on my condition, I reminisced about the last six years of my life. They had passed by like lightning. It was an almost normal life. How different these years had been from the first two years of my diagnosis with the haemodialysis in the hospital; the cruel diet and fluid restrictions, the needles and the failed transplant. Compared to that, the PD phase was pure bliss. It was almost as if I did not have kidney disease. I ate and drank what I liked. I worked. I took holidays. It was a normal life.

'How much more time is Dr Georgi going to take?'

'We don't know, sir. He said he is on his way.'

I went back to the waiting area. It was the beginning of summer in Chennai and the waiting area had one humble fan, which did not suffice as it was getting hot.

PD had given me my life back. And to think I had expected Dr Sastry to refuse to let me try it! And now, again, my life seemed to be on the brink. Dr Abraham was the expert in PD. If anyone could figure this out, it was him. He had done a lot of research on the subject. More than that, he was passionate about it. He genuinely cared for his patients. You could see that in the way he talked to them. His patients also loved him.

They also trusted him with their lives. For them, his was the last word. They needed no more discussions. And now, I found myself outside the court of the judge who would deliver the verdict. What was it going to be?

'Doctor has come.' There was a flurry of activity near the reception of Dr Georgi Abraham's consulting room. The doctor had arrived. This was the second time I was going to be meeting him. There was still some time, though. A few people were to see him before they would show me in.

This was a crucial meeting. We were going to ask him if we could remove the catheter and wait for a few more months. Would the adhesions clear out and would I be able to go back on PD again? I was anxious. How would this meeting end? Would there be hope for the future? Or would it be back to haemodialysis? I could take a few more sessions of it, if there was the promise of returning to PD later. All this was running through my mind as I entered Dr Georgi's room.

'Good evening, doctor.'

I settled down and explained to the good doctor how the Extraneal solution had not worked. He heard me out without mentioning a word. I then asked him the question.

'Can we remove this catheter and wait for a few months, maybe even a year? Then, can we expect the adhesions to clear out? Is there hope that I can go back to PD?'

'No. This will not happen. The adhesions will not clear out. You will need to go back to haemodialysis.'

There it was. The verdict was out.

He did not use too many words. He did not give me any false hope. There wasn't any point in doing so. There was not much I could say. I felt like I was collapsing into the ground, sinking into an abyss. We thanked the doctor and walked out. No one spoke a word. My dad knew how much PD meant to me. He was shocked as well.

We returned to Hyderabad that evening and scheduled the surgery to remove the PD catheter.

That was the end of PD for me, the end of six years of normality. The years I spent on PD were by far the best during my entire time with kidney disease until then. The entire process of haemodialysis is so violent. Blood is drawn out of the body and passed through a machine. PD, in contrast, is much less risky as a process. There are risks of infection, which can sometimes be fatal. But if you follow all the procedures with no laxity and steer clear of tsunamis, PD can be fantastic.

I am a travel freak. With PD, I could travel unfettered. No worrying about getting back in time for my haemo session. I could carry my bags with me or have them delivered to a nearby location. And then, I could stay there for as long as I liked.

With haemodialysis, however, I could go to a place for more than a couple of days, only if there was a dialysis centre there. Even if there was a centre, I was never sure of the quality or if the staff were any good.

Some people I met after the tsunami tell me how lucky I was to be part of a historical event. But for me, the tsunami marked a turning point in my life. I had to give up PD because of the tsunami.

Were the series of PD infections really caused by the tsunami? No one knows. They argue saying the infection started three months after the tsunami. So, it could not be. Maybe I had become a little lax with sterile procedures during my PD exchanges. While I did the exit site dressings with the utmost care, I might have just taken some liberties with my exchange procedures. Could this have caused me to lose the ability to do PD?

Whatever it was, life had changed forever. I would need to go back on haemodialysis and be on that modality for a while. How long? I had no clue. It could be forever.

It was time to test my mental strength yet again. Would I survive? Would I succumb? How would I cope with the devastation that the tsunami brought about in my life? Even if it may not have caused the PD infection, the timing couldn't have been more symbolic. A storm had struck and destroyed my life. I had to begin my life afresh. I had to pick up the pieces that were left and build my life again. Much like the survivors of the tsunami.

* * *

6

Taking the Uncharted Path

'It matters not how strait the gate,
How charged with punishments the scroll,
I am the master of my fate,
I am the captain of my soul.'

—William Ernest Henley

I was not happy about haemodialysis in the hospital.

Most patients undergo haemodialysis in a dialysis centre thrice a week for between three and five hours each time. In India, most people get four-hour sessions twice a week. Only about a third do it thrice a week. Compare this with the functioning of a kidney. A kidney functions seven days a week and twenty-four hours every day. So, this type of dialysis is inadequate.

Because of this intermittent cleansing of the blood, patients undergo a yo-yo-like effect. Continuous ups and downs. Once they complete their dialysis session, their blood is partially clean, and they have got rid of the excess fluid. But until the next dialysis session, life is a constant struggle. Drink less water. Watch your potassium. Don't have too much fruit.

Energy levels are horrible. After a dialysis session, patients feel a 'crash'. This is a term used to describe the horrible feeling after dialysis. You feel weak, tired, listless and drained.

I could do nothing after dialysis. I would lie on the bed and doze off.

Though I continued working at Effigent, I could not do much. I spent less time at work. Even when I was there, I would not feel like doing much. Life was a struggle.

I was a non-compliant patient. I guess many of us are like that. If the doctor restricts our fluid intake, fluids are all we want to have. I started craving fruits and liquids like crazy.

My weight gain between treatments would be at least 4 kgs. Removing 4 kgs in four hours can tax the body. The crash after dialysis is because of this.

The dialysis process itself was horrible. Lying down in bed for four hours with nothing to do can be very frustrating. With every passing minute, you feel worse because fluid is being removed at such a high rate. All around, you see people feeling miserable. The entire experience can be quite distressing.

I was lucky if I managed to get an hour or two of sleep. The rest of the time would be spent just waiting for the session to finish. Time would move so slowly. It was almost as if the entire world had slowed down.

Around September 2005, I became severely anaemic. Dr Narayen upped my erythropoietin dose. I also had to take iron injections intravenously. But the anaemia persisted.

We then got some more tests done. Nothing seemed unusual. We even got the bone marrow analysed by doing a bone marrow aspiration. That result also was normal.

We consulted a haematologist on Dr Narayen's recommendation. He could not offer us any more answers.

I also developed a persistent cough around this time. X-rays and other regular tests yielded nothing significant. The nephrologist at KIMS, Dr V.S. Reddy, suggested I get an echocardiogram. The echo showed I had left ventricular hypertrophy. This is a condition that dialysis patients get because of the constant fluid overload in their bodies and the rapid fluid removal during the four-hour sessions.

Dr Girish Narayen asked me to see a cardiologist. The cardiologist put me on medication for the heart.

These were all side effects of the regular, in-hospital thrice-a-week dialysis regime. Not having the body's native kidneys can cause so many problems. No one realizes that the kidneys contribute so much to our well-being. Not having them function can affect every part of the body.

It was clear that hospital-based haemodialysis was taking a toll on me. Mentally, I was feeling horrible. And then, it had also affected my heart. While I was continuing to get haemodialysis at KIMS, my primary nephrologist continued to be Dr Girish Narayen. I would visit him regularly for a review. On one such visit, realizing that I was unhappy with regular haemodialysis, Dr Narayen suggested that I try daily home haemodialysis. I asked him how anyone could do that. He explained that one needed to set up a machine at home and then carry out dialysis at night. Frequent, longer duration dialysis provides for an excellent quality of life. I went home thinking about this new thing that I had heard. How could anyone do haemodialysis at home?

I started looking it up on the Internet and found a lot of positive things being said about this modality. I started digging deeper. I found people on the Internet, especially through a website called Home Dialysis Central, who were doing home haemodialysis. Many people spoke about it in glowing terms. Their life had changed after switching to home haemodialysis. There were several posts on mailing lists and forums on the Internet.

It appeared that daily, nocturnal dialysis—seven to eight hours every night, five to six nights a week—offered the best outcomes in terms of well-being, longevity, minimizing co-morbidities (side effects of kidney disease like heart conditions, etc.). The next best was short daily dialysis—two to four hours every day, six to seven days a week). The worst was the four-hour, thrice a week regimen.

One major advantage of doing home haemodialysis in the US was the availability of the NxStage System One machine. This was a portable, small-sized machine, specially designed for home use by patients themselves. The machine was not available in India.

While I could not find any references to daily home haemodialysis being done in India, I found that there were a tiny number of people doing dialysis at home. But those were only the regular, twice- or thrice-a-week sessions. They used the regular, large, hospital machines.

Also, in the US, the infrastructure to manage emergencies was excellent. In fact, some centres also had online monitoring of the dialysis treatment performed at home.

Here, in India, of course, no such infrastructure was present. That was one risk. But I thought I could get a dialysis technician to come home and do the treatment for me. The dialysis technician at KIMS, the hospital I was undergoing dialysis at, was an expert at his work.

I thought this through from various angles. I thought about the pros and cons. There was no one I could contact who was doing daily dialysis in India. So, I could not get first-hand information about the Indian situation. This was quite unnerving.

I realized I did not want to continue the way I was receiving treatment. I could not tolerate my current treatment regimen and needed a better life.

I decided to go for it.

* * *

To make the transition as smooth as possible, I first did short daily dialysis in the hospital. I would go from Monday to Saturday every day for two hours. This was to get used to the idea of dialysing daily. I started this modality in KIMS, Secunderabad, the hospital where I was getting the regular thrice-a-week, four-hour sessions.

I would go for a session every morning at around 7 a.m., get two hours of dialysis and then go to work after that.

All this while, my anaemia showed no signs of improving. Dr Narayen suggested one day that I should consider switching to another dialysis centre. Sometimes, the RO water in the hospital could cause that kind of anaemia in some patients, he said.

I moved to Medwin Hospital. This was the same hospital where I had got admitted in the early days of kidney disease, back in 1997. I continued the same two-hour sessions every morning there as well.

Within a few days of starting dialysis in Medwin, one doctor there asked me to get my viral markers checked.

Dialysis centres test viral markers in dialysis patients to look for the hepatitis C, hepatitis B and HIV viruses. Since the blood of dialysis patients is exposed for several hours a week and there are added complexities such as reprocessing of dialysers and blood lines, where additional contamination can occur, it is important to know if someone has been infected with one of these viruses. This was more to prevent other patients from getting infected rather than to help the patient who may have been infected. By taking some precautions such as moving the patient to get dialysis in a 'positive area' where all infected patients are treated; reprocessing their equipment in a separate enclosure and so on, they can avoid further cross-infections.

I sent my blood for these tests.

The reports came back positive for hepatitis C. They were negative for hepatitis B and HIV. How had this happened? Hepatitis C is a virus that damages the liver over time. It does not cause any symptoms in the short term, but, over fifteen to twenty years, if left untreated, it can cause liver cirrhosis and liver cancer. At that point, unless the liver is replaced, the patient may soon die.

I dashed off to meet Dr Girish Narayen.

As he took the reports in his hands and noticed the results, his eyebrows arched upwards in shock. 'How did this happen?' he asked. He took off his spectacles and rubbed his hand over the length of his face. 'I wish you had not moved to Medwin.'

'Does this mean it happened there, doctor?'

'It looks like that.'

He asked me to meet a hepatologist and wrote a note to Dr P.N. Rao, a hepatologist who worked at Care Hospital, another famous corporate hospital in Hyderabad.

Dr Rao examined me and asked me to get the genotype and viral load. The hepatitis C virus comes in multiple variants. At that time, the known variants were genotypes 1, 2, 3 and 4. The viral load showed how many cells of the virus are present in the blood. They report it in copies per millilitre.

My genotype came back as 3, while my viral load was in millions. There was a drug combination available that had a 50 per cent chance of treating the disease, but the side effects were terrible. Dr Rao advised us to wait until better drugs became available.

In the short term, nothing much would happen. The hepatitis C virus is an indolent virus. It does minimal damage in the short term. In healthy patients, they expect major complications in fifteen to twenty years. In dialysis patients, this could be eight to ten years.

There is a stigma associated with infectious diseases in India. With little awareness of how diseases spread, people make all kinds of assumptions and have unreasonable apprehensions about people afflicted with them. While HIV has the most amount of stigma associated with it, hepatitis B and hepatitis C come next.

Within dialysis centres, patients who had hepatitis C were grouped together as 'positive patients'. They had to get dialysis on specially designated machines on which the 'negative patients' would not get treated. The machines would often be put in separate rooms.

I felt bad about the fact that I was now one among 'positive patients'. I did not like getting dialysis from separate machines. All this for no fault of mine. Some technician messed up somewhere. I had to pay for the lapse on their part.

While there was no immediate danger, I would have to live with this stigma for some time. I had to continue to follow my plan to switch to home haemodialysis. That would solve many problems.

* * *

I moved back to KIMS because I was just not comfortable continuing my dialysis at Medwin, given what had just happened. I continued the two-hours-each-morning routine.

I had to find out more about home haemodialysis and go ahead with this modality that promised to change my life. I did a lot of research about the dialysis machine and the RO plant, the two key pieces of equipment required for home haemodialysis.

A portable haemodialysis machine, such as the NxStage System One, that many people in the US used with excellent results, would have been the best choice. You could carry it along with you when you travelled. Conventional haemodialysis machines used in hospitals are about the size of a mid-sized refrigerator, with a big RO plant fixed to the ground.

However, the NxStage machine could not yet be sold outside the US. Even if I somehow bought it and brought it to India, servicing and repairs would be an issue. I would also have to import specially designed consumables that would be used with it regularly. If something went wrong with the machine, there were no engineers in India who had the ability and training to repair it. I realized that I would have to go with the conventional machine.

I got to know around that time that there were a few people doing home haemodialysis in Mumbai. They were not doing it daily, but about two to three times a week for four hours. I thought it would be useful to see the set-up and talk to them to get a first-hand account of how it was.

I travelled to Mumbai and visited three homes which had the set-up. The condition of the patients wasn't impressive. However, I think the fundamental problem was that they were all doing dialysis at a lower frequency compared to the daily sessions I was planning. I also spoke to a technician who was going to a patient's home to do their dialysis. During our conversation, one thing that he said stood out.

'The major advantage of doing home haemodialysis,' he said, ' was that there are no chances of cross-infections.' I realized then that had I started this a few months earlier, I would not have contracted the hepatitis C virus.

We got back to Hyderabad.

I spoke next to Jayaram, the lead technician at KIMS, about coming home every day to do my dialysis.

Short, fair, with a moustache, Jayaram thrived on his capabilities. He managed the entire dialysis centre at KIMS on his own. The nephrologist there, Dr V.S. Reddy, was sure that Jayaram would take care of everything in the dialysis centre. He could handle all complications; would train his juniors to do basic stuff and maintained tight control of the inventory and operations.

For nephrologists, dialysis is not an exciting part of their professional lives. There is not much to do. They are more interested in kidney transplants, acute kidney injuries and pre-end-stage kidney disease care. These areas are intellectually stimulating. Dialysis does not need too much of thought.

It is often routine problems that need routine solutions. That is why most nephrologists visit a dialysis centre only once or twice a day, just to check if their patients are having any problems that need attention. They spend the rest of their time on more challenging cases.

This leaves management of the dialysis centres to the staff. Often the senior-most technician becomes like the be-all of their empire, the dialysis centre. The patients are their subjects. They all try to be in the technician's good books. They pay their taxes on time. For some, it is sweet boxes. For others, it could be chicken biryani. But everyone tries hard to please the monarch.

God forbid if someone upsets them. They would banish the said miscreant from the kingdom, who would have to look for another dialysis centre or settle for inconvenient dialysis slots.

These chief technicians make most of their income from their side business of injections.

People on dialysis need an injection called erythropoietin. Most people would need to take at least one injection weekly. Most would also need to take iron injections periodically.

Pharmaceutical pricing is one of the most dysfunctional areas in the dialysis value chain. Most pharmaceutical companies set the maximum retail price (MRP) of pharmaceuticals like erythropoietin and iron at more than double of what they usually sell it at. This enables them to give generous discounts and incentives to various stakeholders like dialysis technicians.

Many dialysis technicians make more money than their actual salary through this side business of injections. There is an unholy nexus between pharmaceutical company sales representatives and technicians in the dialysis ecosystem.

Pharmaceutical sales representatives typify the ugly underbelly of medicine in India. Given targets to achieve, these sales reps, as people call them, resort to several unethical and illegal means to achieve them.

Sales reps set up a relationship with dialysis technicians and some doctors too. They offer inducements to prescribe their brand of injections to patients and offer high incentives to do this. Technicians tell patients that they can get them the injection at a huge discount on the MRP if they buy it through them.

The unsuspecting patient thinks that they are at the receiving end of a huge favour. What they do not realize is that they are only pawns in this game. Money is most important in this game and no one does anyone any favours.

Jayaram had grown the KIMS Dialysis Centre from a few machines to one of the largest centres in the city. He was an expert in everything related to dialysis. All the staff and the patients looked up to him and held him in great esteem.

I requested Jayaram to help me with my home haemodialysis.

Jayaram was one of the primary reasons why I opted for home haemodialysis. While the idea was Dr Girish Narayen's, if it wasn't for Jayaram, I would not have embarked on the journey. It was just too daunting. It was too scary. No one was doing daily nocturnal home haemo. What if something went wrong? There was no ICU or emergency care at home.

Jayaram gave me the confidence that if anything should go wrong, he could handle it. The way he managed emergencies in the hospital made me confident that he could handle things at home. Then there was his sheer confidence and attitude. He had seen several cases and had tremendous experience dealing with such incidents. In an emergency, experience counts far more than education.

The way Jayaram had grown in the field of dialysis was remarkable. He is testament to the thinking that often, in the storm of life, it is the experience of steering the ship rather than knowing the internals of its engine that can help you get to the shore. Despite not having a formal degree in dialysis, he was far better than even the highly educated in this field. He could handle complications and cannulate deep, twisted-vein fistulae with ease.

Complication handling is one of the most important aspects that staff in a dialysis centre need to be familiar with. Proper management of complications can sometimes mean the difference between life and death for a dialysis patient. Dialysis is a complex process. So many changes are happening in the body that are very unphysiological—that the body is not used to—that it does not know how to handle them. So, it can react in very dangerous ways. Technicians need to manage these problems and ensure that they restore stability in the body. This can come only with years of careful observation and learning.

I had myself seen several serious complications take place at the KIMS Dialysis Centre. Jayaram was the only one in the centre who could manage these incidents. He would do it with such a calm demeanour that everyone around would be sure that he was going to save the day. From a serious case of convulsions to several cardiac arrests, Jayaram had it covered. So, when I thought of doing home haemodialysis, I was very sure that it had to be Jayaram who would be there to do my dialysis. I would be safe under his care.

* * *

Around this time, I got to know, through online sources again, about buttonhole needles. This was a new technique often used in home haemodialysis where blunt needles are used instead of sharp ones.

For many haemodialysis patients, the worst part about the process is the insertion of two thick needles in the arm that facilitate continuous drawing out of blood and its return to the body after purification in the artificial kidney. Typically, in successive sessions, needles are inserted pretty close to the old point of insertion. After three to four sessions, the first point of insertion is reused. A step-ladder-like pattern forms on the skin from the repeated puncturing.

To reduce the pain associated with the needles, someone came up with the concept of using blunt needles. First, a tract forms in the flesh by pricking at the same point during five to six successive dialysis sessions. Subsequently, a blunt needle is used for cannulation that goes through this tract with little pain. This technique is called the buttonhole method.

I wanted to try this.

I contacted the company in the US, Medisystems, that was manufacturing these needles. They needed a doctor to prescribe it and could not sell it to anyone just like that. I got Obul's (who was the founder of Effigent) wife Neeraja (a nephro-pathologist at Stanford University in California, US) to write out a prescription. They delivered the needles to her, and someone coming to India over the next few days brought them for me.

As I was mortified by the pain from cannulation, I was excited about this.

I explained the technique to Jayaram and asked him to cannulate at the same sites for the next six dialysis sessions. In the seventh session, I asked him to use the blunt needle. It went through without any effort and I felt almost no pain.

This technique made life on dialysis a little less unpleasant. I usually required a mild local anaesthetic before cannulation with sharp needles. I did not need this any more.

Sometimes, if I looked somewhere else during cannulation, I would not even know that the needle was going in.

There are several other benefits to this technique. Many patients who've been on dialysis for long develop swelling in their veins under the skin, and this makes the arm with the fistula look quite ugly. This rarely happened with buttonhole needles. Already, a part of my vein had swollen and made my upper left arm look

ugly. After I switched to these needles, I did not get any more
swelling in my veins.

Another problem with sharp needles was that, sometimes, the
needle could go right through the entire vein and puncture the
other wall. It would lead to severe pain and blood leaking out and
collecting under the skin. This was impossible with buttonhole
needles because the needle tips were blunt and could not tear
open a vein wall unless there was a well-established tract.

There was, however, a risk that was documented in literature
related to the use of buttonhole needles. It was associated with an
increased incidence of access-related infections. Several patients
had their fistula sites infected. This was primarily because of the
same sites being used again and again without being provided the
opportunity to heal. Sometimes, these infections got out of hand
and spread elsewhere.

Because of this risk, some dialysis centres in the US had
stopped using this technique altogether. Many nephrologists were
also sceptical and would not recommend it to their patients.

I was mindful of these risks and continued this technique.

All my research on home haemodialysis had been conducted
online. I found that many patients on home haemodialysis were
cannulating themselves. Cannulation was the most feared part of
haemodialysis.

In many dialysis centres, patients get used to one technician
cannulating them. This helps both patient and technician because
the technician gets used to the patient's fistula and knows the
depth at which it is located and the direction the vein is in. This
makes their job easy. The patient is also comfortable because they
are assured that the cannulation is going to be trouble-free.[1]

The trouble is that the patient becomes dependent on
one technician. If that technician is on leave or in another
shift, then the patient dreads another technician attempting to
cannulate them.

The best solution to this problem, according to the online forums I was a part of, was to cannulate yourself. Since you are always going to be there for your own dialysis, all you need to do is to learn to cannulate one fistula and your life will be trouble-free as far as cannulation is concerned. This made sense.

So, one day, I discussed this with Jayaram. He was fully supportive. Under his guidance, I successfully cannulated myself. The buttonhole needles made it much easier because there was already a tract. All you had to do was nudge the needle down the tract.

I have never been cannulated by someone else after that. Both buttonholing and self-cannulation were things I got started with during my sessions in KIMS Hospital before I began home haemodialysis.

Cannulating yourself gives you a tremendous amount of confidence. You no longer depend on any 'good' technician for your dialysis. Though putting two thick needles in your arm may seem very counter-intuitive, it is the most logical solution to the problem of cannulation pain during dialysis.

* * *

I had to buy the equipment needed for home haemodialysis. After speaking to several doctors, patients and technicians, I decided to go with the Fresenius 4008S, a sturdy machine that was the most widely used in India. I also bought an Ion Exchange RO plant. The haemodialysis machine was set up in my bedroom while the RO plant was installed on the terrace of my two-storey house. The necessary electrical and plumbing work had been done. An RO water connection had been provided in my bedroom for the HD machine and in my bathroom for the cleaning of the tubes and dialyser after dialysis.

Everything was finally ready, and we planned to start on 13 May 2006.

I decided to go for short daily at home to begin with and then, when things settled down, switch to nocturnal. I was already doing short daily at the hospital. So, clinically, there would be no difference.

With Jayaram's connections, I got the consumables from different suppliers. I felt indebted to Jayaram for connecting me to them.

My parents, the team that set up the infrastructure and Jayaram were all at home the first day. Jayaram set everything up. Within about half an hour, I was on dialysis.

My first short daily session went off without any problems. I dialysed for two hours. I continued short daily dialysis (except Sundays) for about twenty days. There were no problems at all. My father would switch on the RO plant on the terrace every morning and switch it off when it was full. Jayaram would come after his shift at KIMS, and I would get a two-hour-long session.

I then felt that things were going well enough for us to switch to nocturnal. Jayaram was ready. The first night, I thought I wouldn't get any sleep at all. I ended up sleeping like I hadn't slept for days. My eyes opened only when the machine beeped to signal completion of the treatment in the morning.

We slowly settled into a routine. Jayaram would come at around 10 p.m. He would set up the machine and everything else that was needed. I would cannulate myself. Once the session began, we would watch some television. He would sleep in the same room to take care of any alarms and problems that would come up. The treatment would end at around 5 a.m. and he would disconnect me and leave.

There were hardly any alarms from the machine throughout the night. Most of them needed a 'Reset' button press to take care of. There were, however, some mildly serious problems.

Sometimes, blood would ooze from my arterial and venous sites. Jayaram could handle all these emergencies with his expertise. These incidents were because I would end up moving my hands while sleeping that would cause the needles to move and therefore the oozing. We then decided to tie my finger in a manner that would allow some movement for my arm, but not enough to cause any oozing.

Once we did this, the oozing stopped completely.

* * *

I started learning all the processes involved. At first, I just learned how to mix the bicarbonate solution that is used with the acid solution to create the dialysate. This was trivial. You just needed to get the proportions right. Then, I learned how to prime the dialyser and tubing before dialysis. This was not too difficult either. For a long time, I used to prepare the bicarb solution and finish the priming before Jayaram came and he would come and start dialysis.

Subsequently, I also learned to start the dialysis session myself. Preparing the bicarb solution, priming, cannulation and then starting dialysis by connecting the tubes to the needles and initiating the process. I felt confident when I started doing this as I had learnt a complex set of processes that affected my health and I could do it with no help.

At one point, I would start the session myself and an hour or more of dialysis would be complete before Jayaram came. The toughest part about starting dialysis is putting the tapes on the needles after cannulation. You have only one hand to do this, since the other arm is what you are working on. I figured out hacks to make it easy.

Most of the time, things would go without any problem. On one day, though, the machine kept beeping continuously. I also found the blood in the blood line becoming dark. I checked everything that I assumed might have gone wrong, but could not find the source of the problem. Luckily, Jayaram entered just then and found that I had forgotten to release the clamp on the line that connected to the venous needle which returned blood to my body. This was causing blood to build up in the line while the blood pump was running, causing all kinds of issues. As soon as he unclamped the line, the machine stopped sounding the alarm.

Such instances were very few, and mostly, things went on well. I settled into a routine and stabilized on the health front. Daily nocturnal home haemodialysis gave me my life back once more, especially after the normal years on peritoneal dialysis.

There were no diet and fluid restrictions. Since I was getting seven to eight hours of dialysis, I could remove a lot more fluid. As much as 3–4 litres could be removed in one session without any complications. Few people can drink more than that in about sixteen hours, which is the time between two dialysis sessions.

I began feeling better than what I did when I was on dialysis in the hospital. My energy levels were much better. I went back to work full time and would put in about eight to ten hours of productive work every day.

I also started going for a swim every morning. That soon became the best part of my day. This was something I had missed when I was on PD too. I was very glad to resume swimming, something I had not done from the time I was diagnosed with kidney disease.

My haemoglobin levels improved and became normal. I did not need erythropoietin injections any more. The left ventricular hypertrophy that I had developed more than a year ago also got resolved with no change in medication. The cardiologist was surprised to see this and said it was probably because of the daily dialysis. He hadn't seen this happen in regular dialysis patients at all in his entire career.

Travel was an issue, though. When I would travel, I could not do my regular nocturnal sessions. That restricted travel plans to being away from home for a maximum of two nights. I could be away for more nights, but I needed to do one or more regular four-hour hospital dialysis sessions when I was away. I didn't like those sessions at all because I could not sleep during the daytime sessions and also had to watch my fluid and food.

So, it was mostly 'back to normal' for me, something I had only experienced during my years on PD.

I also got treated for hepatitis C. After one unsuccessful attempt, I took a new class of drugs classified as direct-acting agents, a breakthrough in the treatment of this disease. I was able to get rid of the virus by taking a drug of this type.

I had overcome the third major challenge life had thrown at me. Every time I faced a trial, life would offer a solution. I feel so grateful for this. First, it was the initial diagnosis of kidney disease and all the failed alternate therapies. A kidney transplant offered hope at that point. When the kidney transplant failed, I got to know about peritoneal dialysis. And when the tsunami brought about the end of PD for me, it was home haemodialysis.

I know several patients who died in each of the above stages. Many kidney patients in India die before they can get diagnosed. Several get diagnosed but die before they can get treated, either because of their inability to afford or get access to treatment. Several start off on treatments but die because of poor quality of treatment or their inability to cope with the emotional and physical burden that the disease brings along. I have been very lucky to have a family and the resources to get good quality treatment that enabled me to lead a normal life despite being diagnosed at such an early age.

* * *

Towards the second half of 2007, inspired by a colleague at Effigent, Akbar Pasha, I started writing a blog. Blogging was fairly new to India at that time. Not too many blogs existed. Akbar had a blog where he wrote about different things, mostly introspective posts around self-improvement. The idea of letting the world read your thoughts and opinions was very intriguing. I decided to start my blog and set up an account with Blogger, the blogging platform that Google provided. I simply called it Kamal Shah's Blog, which was the default name Blogger suggested.

My first post was about my journey with kidney disease. It had been just over ten years and this was an excellent opportunity to recount the journey. I started blogging about different topics— food, religion, politics. The aspects related to dialysis, however, touched a chord with several people. The blog became fairly popular among patients and others involved in nephrology such as doctors, technicians, nurses and so on.

In my posts related to dialysis, the emphasis was mostly around leading a normal life even while on dialysis. Home HD had given me my life back. I wanted to spread the message that dialysis did not mean the end of life. I had seen several patients around me when I was on hospital haemodialysis. They seemed so miserable. They were frustrated and depressed all the time.

I had realized during those last few years that it did not need to be like that. It was possible to lead a life that was close to normal. I had myself experienced such a life. My years on PD were pure bliss. No one could tell I was on dialysis unless I told them. Then, there was a brief period of turbulence when I had to deal with the infections due to PD. Soon though, that storm settled and I got on to home haemodialysis. Calm returned yet again.

Each time, I took matters in my own hands and looked for options. I grabbed opportunities when I got them and did not take things lying down. I wanted the best care for myself and I ensured

I got it. Always being proactive about my health, I talked openly to my doctors.

I realized that not everyone was like me. I saw people becoming so submissive to the disease that it felt as if they had become slaves and did as it commanded. They had lost all the will to fight and were simply carrying along until death came as a welcome relief from the suffering, both for them and their families.

And yet, it needn't have been that way.

This message had to be spread. How? The blog was a straightforward way. In those days, when blogs were not as common as they are today, my blog became fairly popular. I had set up a Google Analytics account which showed me how many people were visiting the blog, and I could see that the number was steadily rising. I started getting comments on the posts. Most were from people I did not even know. People started asking me questions about various aspects of kidney disease. Some asked for medical advice. Some asked for financial help.

I avoided answering any medical questions, politely telling them they should check with their doctor and that I was not a doctor. I also directed people who asked for financial help to some trusts that I knew helped dialysis patients. The questions I liked to answer the most were around lifestyle with dialysis. There were questions on travel, diet, work, exercise, on home haemodialysis, self-cannulation, etc. I answered all of them to the best of my knowledge.

I became good friends with some people who kept coming back to my blog. Some would send me an email for a more detailed conversation. Some would request my phone number. I, too, would volunteer and share my number for a call to have a more meaningful discussion. There is a limit to what you can discuss over email.

I am in touch with several readers of my blog even today and have formed strong bonds with some of them. Having met them several times, I have had meals and also shared joys and sorrows with them. The support often became a two-way thing. When I was down, they would cheer me up. When they were frustrated with something, I would try to reduce their sorrow.

The blog turned out to be therapeutic for me. It was a form of release. I would pour my heart out at times; try to bring a smile at other times. It was almost like an online diary, only that it was open to the world.

I realized the impact my blog was creating only several years later. One evening, at a family dinner, a distant cousin remarked that her friend had spoken to her about someone on dialysis who was helping spread hope and positivity among other patients. When she dug further, she realized that it was her own cousin, me!

My blog was also mentioned at a nephrology conference by Dr Sundar Sankaran, a very senior nephrologist from Bengaluru. Dr Sundar was speaking at the conference and during the talk, he recommended that all nephrologists read my blog.

Little did I know that the blog was going to open up a new world for me in the future. I had no clue of the massive impact that the blog would have in the years to come. A few words penned on my laptop would alter the course of my life. My writings would bring meaning to my life. I would find my calling and my life would never be the same again.

* * *

7

I Had a Dream

'I have a dream, a song to sing
To help me cope, with anything.
If you see the wonder, of a fairy tale
You can take the future, even if you fail.'

—Benny Andersson/
Björn K. Ulvaeus, ABBA

I had made several friends in the US and other countries from the Home Dialysis Central website and forums on the Internet. So, I was very excited when I got to know in late 2009 that some home haemodialysis patients in the US who were using the portable NxStage home haemo machine were going on a cruise with their dialysis machines!

To me, a luxury cruise was the ultimate holiday. I imagined a massive city on sea. Huge decks adorned with swimming pools. Auditoriums with fantastic performances. Restaurants serving myriad foods. Rooms overlooking the ocean. I wanted to go! The only thing I had seen close to this was in the film *Titanic*.

I emailed Rich Berkowitz and Bill Peckham, both long-term nocturnal home haemo patients in the US who were coordinating the cruise. I asked if I could come as well. They were delighted to know I wanted to join them. There were several hurdles, however. This was a cruise where NxStage patients were taking their machines on board.

Slight problem: I didn't have a NxStage machine.

In the US, patients don't pay for their dialysis or their machines for home haemo. They are covered by private insurance or Medicare (a government-funded healthcare programme). So those who want to do home haemo don't have to buy a machine or pay for the consumables. It is all funded. They only have to cough up a co-pay, usually a small amount compared to the cost of the treatment.

Indians and much of the rest of the developing world cannot afford such luxuries.

So, the machine would have to be sourced out. They figured that if I somehow got a machine, the training to use it could be shortened to a week since I was already dialysing at home and cannulating myself. The normal training programme for a naïve patient is about six weeks.

I got in touch with a company called Satellite Healthcare, which was a non-profit dialysis provider. I wrote to someone through a common friend and asked them if I could rent a NxStage machine for the cruise. They had never received such a request. All their patients were funded by health insurance schemes and they were not used to letting out machines for individuals who paid directly.

However, I could sense a genuine desire to help and that made me hopeful while I realized that the chances of success were minuscule. I exchanged several emails with the team. They were trying their best.

After a couple of weeks, I got an email from them saying that they could rent a machine for me along with the consumables. However, they would need me to pay the equivalent of two full months of rent and whatever I needed for the sessions themselves. This was because the cruise started towards the end of the month and went into the next month. The cost was prohibitive. It would be more than the cost of the rest of my entire trip, which included flights and the cruise itself. At that point, I decided I would not do it.

I emailed Rich and Bill and let them know that I was dropping my plans. They were as disappointed as I was. I followed Bill's blog during the cruise and felt bad about the fact that for no fault of mine, I couldn't join this historic trip. A bunch of lively dialysis patients were making the most of life despite their crippling illness and showed the world that they could lead fulfilling and fun-filled lives.

The longing to go on a luxury cruise never left me, though.

Cut to mid-2011.

My college friends, Chetan, Dinesh, and my namesake, Kamal, and I had been planning a reunion forever. Somehow, things never materialized. These were friends who I was very close to, my best buddies. Chetan Suryanarayana worked for Indian IT giant, Infosys, in Dallas in the US. Dinesh Murthy worked for Microsoft in Seattle and Kamal Kumar worked for a company called Fibre Glass Pilkington in Calgary, Canada. We had gone on a trip together during our last year in college. Inspired by O. Henry's short story, 'After Twenty Years', where two friends in college decide to meet at a particular date and time no matter what, the four of us had planned to do the same thing. However, we had set a timeline of ten years as twenty seemed too long. 2007 would have been that year. But one thing or the other came up and the reunion never materialized.

During my regular Internet search, I came across a site called Dialysis at Sea. The company tied up with cruise liners and set up a few dialysis machines along with everything that was needed for dialysis, on the ship. They also had some dialysis technicians and nurses who would be on the ship, along with a nephrologist. They had the wherewithal to dialyse patients on the ship itself.

My cruise dreams came alive again. I felt this was made just for me.

I checked with my friends about this and suggested that we go on a cruise that had tied up with this company. They all agreed. The first step would be the US visa. This was a major problem.

I had quite a history with US visas. My first encounter with a US consulate was way back in July 1997 on the eve of the life-shattering diagnosis. No questions were asked. A simple look at the papers and the words, 'Counter number 4, please', which meant I had to pay the visa fee. Then came the second tryst. This was around 2006. I was with Effigent. I wanted to get on to the NxStage machine and convinced the rest of the Effigent team that I had to move to the US where I would be on the company's payroll and hence, covered by medical insurance, which would in turn take care of the cost of the machine and the consumables. My entire medical expenses would be taken care of. And I would get access to eculizumab[1] and a kidney transplant in the future. Perfect!

I got all my papers ready for the visa and went to the consulate, this time in Hyderabad itself. As I handed over my papers for the L1 (long-term work) visa, the officer asked me some basic questions. He then said they wanted to give me the visa but they had to do some additional verification and that I would have to respond to an email. I got an email that had some pretty routine questions and sent the answers back at once.

About four months after that, I received my passport with the stamped visa. By that time, things had changed quite a bit within the company and I had to stay in India as the operations here needed me more than the US office did.

With all this history in mind, I got started on the visa process. I put all the paperwork together and went for the visa appointment at the US consulate. At the consulate, when my turn came, the officer was cordial and decided to grant me the visa. However, when he was entering the details into the computer, some flag showed up that told him he needed to put my application under 'Administrative Processing'. Not again! He told me they wanted to give me the visa, but there was some additional verification that they would need to do. Deja vu. They would send me a questionnaire by email which I would need to respond to and then wait. They did not know how long it would take.

The whole routine repeated itself. I told my friends what had happened. I told them that it could take months. All plans were put on hold. When I got my visa, depending on cruise options, we would revisit the plans.

My cruise plan seemed jinxed.

After around four months, sure enough, the passport arrived with the visa in place. I told my friends at once. We started looking for cruise options. After a lot of back and forth, we finalized a 22 July 2012 cruise that sailed from Vancouver to Alaska and back. It was a week-long cruise organized by a cruise company called Celebrity.

I decided to go on an extended holiday to the US and Canada. Two weeks after the cruise, I planned to visit Seattle, Los Angeles, San Francisco, Las Vegas, New Jersey, New York and Toronto. I got in touch with DaVita, the second-largest dialysis provider network in the US for all my dialysis sessions in the US after the cruise. Dialysis at Sea would take care of the three dialysis sessions on the ship.

Since the cruise started off from Vancouver, I would need a Canadian visa as well. I looked up the visa document requirements and submitted them. I took the whole thing casually. Since I already had a US visa and was visiting Canada only for a few days, there wouldn't be too much of a problem, or so I thought. I could not have been more wrong. My Canadian visa application was rejected. I applied again. It was rejected again. My entire trip was in jeopardy. I was thinking of cancelling it. My parents thought I should go ahead with the rest of the trip. However, the main reason I had wanted to go on that trip was the cruise.

Another highlight of my trip was going to be the 'Maid of the Mist' ride at Niagara Falls from the Canadian side of the falls. Both of these would not be possible. Again, I felt I should cancel the entire thing.

I let my friends know about this. They were all very disappointed. They discussed among themselves and decided to convince me to give the visa one more shot. This time, they sent their cruise confirmations, and we added a lot more documentation. My friend Kamal Kumar got in touch with the Canadian prime minister's office, who was representing the constituency that Kamal lived in. He found the file notes on my visa file! We got to know the reasons for the refusal and, point by point, addressed the concerns. I also changed the travel agent through whom I submitted my application, choosing a much more professional agent this time.

Within a week of submitting the application, I got my visa!

So, the trip was on. I sent my three buddies an email letting them know.

If it wasn't for them convincing me to apply again, adding for good measure that they would foot the visa application fee, I would never have done it. I would have given up on the cruise. I would have gone ahead with the trip, albeit a short one, without the cruise and the visit to Niagara Falls. It would have been a half-hearted trip. Now, it would be my original itinerary.

One thing that was always at the back of my mind during the planning was that I would get much less than optimal dialysis. It was going to be a three-week trip. I would do some nocturnal sessions in dialysis centres and some regular four-hour sessions. These would also be spaced out with one- or two-day gaps.

This is the part I hate about holidaying while on dialysis. You need to watch your fluid and diet, which seems somewhat ridiculous especially because you are on a holiday.

But I guess it is better than not holidaying at all.

So, I had two fears as the date of the trip approached. One, of course, was fluids. With one- and two-day gaps, would I be able to restrict my fluid intake? This was not the first time I was going to have to restrict my fluid, though, after getting on to nocturnal. I had been on trips to Goa and had got less frequent dialysis there. But the big difference was that those were only four- or five-day trips, whereas this was a whole three weeks.

Second was the fear that with three weeks of non-frequent dialysis, would other uremic symptoms like nausea trouble me?

My trip was divided into four parts. The first leg was when I got to Seattle. There, I would get two continuous days of four-hour sessions. So that would mean that I would have access to good dialysis. The second part would be the cruise itself. I was hoping that I would be so busy having fun on the cruise with my buddies and the shore excursions that I would not have time to even think about the dialysis. Then, would be the California leg— Los Angeles and San Jose—where I would have three alternate night nocturnal sessions, which would mean good dialysis. These should be easy, I thought. Last was the Las Vegas, Toronto and New Jersey leg. Here I had one session each. So, not too bad.

I also thought it would be interesting to see how dialysis was done in other countries as well and compare it to how it was done here in India. I was getting all my dialysis sessions in DaVita centres except in Toronto, where I was going to a private centre, the only one that offered dialysis to international visitors. Initially, I had tried to book all nocturnal sessions, but surprisingly, very few centres had that facility.

I was hoping for my trip to go off well. I was going to be on a holiday that was costing me a lot. This was most likely going to be my only such trip ever, and I wanted things to go perfectly.

* * *

I flew into Seattle a couple of days before the cruise and met my buddies from college and their families. I got two sessions of dialysis at the DaVita centre there. The centre staff respected my ability to self-cannulate and allowed me to set my dialysis parameters.

The ship set sail at around 4.30 p.m. on Sunday, 15 July. We sailed towards Alaska from Vancouver. The cruise ship was like a rich, luxurious city in the ocean.

Alaska is a stunning place. It is the largest state in the US. We made three stops at land in Alaska. Our first stop was called Icy Strait Point and was located off Hoonah, a fishing village in Alaska, where we did a three-hour kayak trip.

The next day, the ship was to go to the Hubbard Glacier. As we neared the glacier, the weather became colder. Along the way to the glacier, we started seeing chunks of ice floating on the water. When we reached the glacier, almost everyone on board gathered on the various decks to get a glimpse of the magnificent structure. We were all on the upper decks, getting pictures and taking in the scene's beauty.

The next stop was Juneau, the capital of Alaska, where we did a river-rafting trip down Mendenhall, the river that gets its water from the Mendenhall Glacier. The last stop was Ketchikan, where we just took a walk around town.

Alaska was probably the most beautiful place I have ever seen in the world. The weather, the natural beauty and the unspoilt surroundings make it a must-see destination.

When we were at sea, we enjoyed the amenities the ship offered, such as the swimming pool, the jacuzzi, the many restaurants and the events they had at the theatre. We also spent a lot of time with each other. It had been fifteen years since we last met.

This week on the cruise was one of the best weeks I have ever had in my life. I fulfilled my dream of going on a cruise ship. I couldn't have asked for a better ship or a better destination. And finally, I couldn't have asked for better company.

During my seven-night cruise, I got three dialysis sessions. Monday, Wednesday and Saturday. The sessions were all uneventful.

While I would have liked to have access to daily nocturnal dialysis on the ship, this was an excellent compromise. The trouble is that you lose out on about five hours of your day, which could have been spent having fun. I also did not like the aggressive dialysis compared to the gentle dialysis I was used to. It made me a little dizzy after the session, which did not allow me to stay up late into the night.

Dialysis at Sea was doing a great job with this. They have made cruising possible for folks on dialysis. This would not have been possible without them. Yes, the charges are high, but at least there is an option.

After the cruise, I spent another couple of weeks in the US visiting Los Angeles, San Francisco, Yosemite National Park, Las Vegas, Toronto, Niagara Falls, New York and New Jersey before heading back home. Among all these places, I enjoyed the trips to Yosemite and Niagara Falls the most. I quite hated Las Vegas and New York. This was quite contrary to what my friends and family had suggested. They had said that Manhattan and Vegas would be the highlight of my trip apart from the cruise. I realized then that I was more of a nature lover than a tall skyscraper and nightlife enthusiast. I wonder how there could be anyone who is a tall skyscraper and nightlife lover.

This trip was a major event in my life. It was the first long trip I ever undertook after being diagnosed with kidney disease. It was also my first-ever trip outside India. Going to the US while on dialysis; getting ten dialysis sessions in various centres there; going on a luxury cruise and getting dialysis onboard, all this was stuff only dreams were made of, at least for me. But it all turned out to be real. This needed a lot of determination. Several challenges arose. One by one, they were overcome. I was fortunate to have tremendous support from my family and friends and the ability to do this from my own savings and not have to dip into any other resources.

Paulo Coelho has said, 'When you want something, all the universe conspires to help you to achieve it.' My US trip was the perfect example of this.

* * *

Part 2

8

Finding My Calling

'There is a tide in the affairs of men, which taken at the flood, leads on to fortune. Omitted, all the voyage of their life is bound in shallows and in miseries. On such a full sea are we now afloat. And we must take the current when it serves, or lose our ventures.'

—William Shakespeare

Effigent soon became a 200-people company with offices in San Jose in California, US and Hyderabad and Bengaluru in India. However, we were always short of funds as we could not gain enough traction in getting good projects that could make the company sustainable. Towards 2008, things became bad with one major project getting shelved and the inability of the US team in getting us enough clients for an ERP product for the Mac that we had built.

At one point, we decided it was best to sell the company. It was a very hard decision for Obul. But it was in his own best interest to do this without incurring further losses. We found a buyer in Prithvi Info Solutions. The founder was a friend of Obul's and was primarily into body shopping (hiring people trained in various aspects of software development and having them work for clients at their offices) from India to the US. He thought it would be an excellent opportunity to take over the business for Apple software-related expertise and clients.

The money received was barely enough to take care of urgent payments. Several founding members who had put in money could get nothing back.

I had lived without a salary for much of the previous year, and started looking for jobs. An opportunity came from a start-up called Grene. They focused on bringing technology into the infrastructure industry. They were building home automation solutions for a sister company that was into constructing high-end homes in Hyderabad. The work was interesting. It was a software development role. It was something I was yearning for. I wanted to be just another guy in the company. I did not want to 'manage' anything.

My tenure at Grene was satisfactory. The work was excellent. The pay helped manage my expenses and also save a little. My bosses and colleagues were all very sweet. They were accommodating of my health needs. This was in stark contrast with several other fellow dialysis patients who got little support from their workplaces.

However, I was always itching to do something in the kidney disease and dialysis space. I had seen everything anyone with kidney failure would see in their lifetime. Knowing what was wrong with the ecosystem, I knew how we could correct it. I always had a doubt at the back of my mind though: would I be able to pull it off alone?

Software development was something that just happened. I was looking to keep busy with something and Hemanti Aunty was kind enough to let me work in her company. While I did my chemical engineering, when I look back at the choices I have made with my career, I clearly see that was a mistake.

In India, peer pressure affects career choices significantly. During my student days, engineering and medicine were picked by those who were good at academics. Commerce was chosen by those who either had a family business or were not good at academics. Well, there were a few exceptions. But this was mostly it.

Arts? What's Arts?

It wasn't even thought of as an option. When I think about what I was truly passionate about, I believe it was English literature and Indian history. Not only did I not mention this to anyone, I did not know it myself. The thought that I could be interested in something other than mathematics (since I hated biology) did not cross my mind even for a fleeting moment. That you picked only one of these two subjects was so deeply ingrained in our minds, we did not even debate over any other options, even with ourselves.

Today, things have changed a little. Ashoka University, one of India's most reputed universities, is dedicated to the liberal arts. I would have loved to study there, given a chance to relive my life.

Now that I had been through a few years of kidney disease, this felt close to my heart. Kidney patients felt like kindred souls. Was there a way I could work in this space and also sustain myself financially?

The way peritoneal dialysis was treated in the country and elsewhere as well always upset me. It was always the step-child of nephrology. I got in touch with Harish Natarajan, who was the head of Baxter's Peritoneal Dialysis division at one time and had, by then, moved on to take on a role with Bausch and Lomb in Singapore. Harish was an IITM/IIMA graduate who had spent several years in leadership positions in healthcare and FMCG

companies. He had a brilliant mind minus the attitude you might
associate with someone with his credentials.

I had been in touch with Harish when I was on PD. I called
him and said I wanted to do something in PD and was even
ready to become a distributor. Confident of the fact that if more
patients got to know about PD, they would opt for it, I started
thinking about how I could start looking for patients who were on
haemodialysis and tell them about the magical world that existed
beyond the haemodialysis unit. A world where there were few diet
and fluid restrictions; where they did not have any needles; where
they were the masters of their own future and, where they did not
have to depend on unscrupulous technicians.

Harish knew the Indian healthcare system better than me.
I did not know how things worked. I just had this romantic idea
of doing something in dialysis and thought I could convince
patients to switch to PD. Harish dissuaded me. Probably laughing
at my naïvety and considering me a fool for thinking it would be
so easy, he promised to put me in touch with Malti Sachdev, who
was his successor at Baxter. He thought I would be a wonderful
fit at Baxter. He wanted me to take up a job with the company.
I wondered, what would I do at a place like that?

I read up a little about Malti Sachdev. She had impressive
credentials. She had quit a regular corporate job at one point and
spent some time working in the social sector. Frustrated with the
lack of proper organization there, she joined Baxter as its head
of renal services in India. I got on a call with Malti and talked to
her about how I felt PD got such a raw deal in India. While she
agreed with me, I felt she was not sure how I would fit into the
company's scheme of things. Things did not go any further.

I gave up all thoughts about doing anything in PD after that
and continued my work at Grene.

Around this time, I developed severe bone pain. The pain was
mainly in my ribs, back and feet. I started limping while walking.

Any sudden jerks or movements would cause a stabbing pain in these areas. I consulted Dr Girish Narayen. He tried different things, but we could not understand what the cause was. We did several tests with inconclusive results. Finally, we discovered I was using a very low calcium dialysate by mistake. Several months ago, my calcium levels had become high. Dr Girish Narayen suggested that I use a slightly low calcium dialysate. Most centres use a 3 mEq/L calcium dialysate. Dr Narayen advised that I use a 2.5 mEq/L dialysate. I realized to my horror that I was using 1.5 mEq/L. This was causing my calcium levels to drop. As a result, the parathyroid hormone[2] levels in my body started shooting up. This caused calcium to be leached from the bones, causing the pain.

I suffered with this pain for almost a year before we figured out the cause and took corrective action. Even after taking necessary action, it was a good two to three months before the pain abated.

People wonder why I did not sue the company that provided the dialysate chemical. The trouble in India is that these things are not that simple. First, there was no written instruction from me asking for 2.5 mEq/L calcium. I did it orally, over a phone call. Second, we can never prove beyond doubt that the bone pain was because of the wrong dialysate.

That sums up the healthcare scenario in India. Poor service, zero accountability.

* * *

On the afternoon of 28 August 2009, I received an email from someone called Vikram Vuppala. He said he had stumbled upon my blog and spent a couple of hours going through it. He had a close relative, an uncle, who died of kidney failure. He wondered if we could meet up for breakfast at a place of my choice over the next few days to discuss the topic. I was always ready to talk about the kidney disease space in India. I was already in touch, over email, phone and in person as well, with several patients and their families looking for advice from a patient who had experienced it all. This was a topic close to my heart. I would always make time for it.

A couple of days later, we met in Secunderabad's Belson's Taj Mahal Hotel. Vikram was already there when I reached. He was in his early thirties, about five and a half feet tall. Vikram grew up in Hyderabad. He did his engineering from the reputed Indian Institute of Technology in Kharagpur and then his master of science from the University of Illinois. He then worked as a business analyst in ZS Associates and at Abbott Laboratories and did his MBA from the acclaimed Booth School in Chicago. After passing out from Booth in 2007, he joined McKinsey before moving back to India after a very fulfilling ten-odd years in the US. He wanted to start something of his own in healthcare and had four ideas he was considering and had done research on. One of these ideas was a dialysis network. While researching about dialysis in India, he had come across my blog and got in touch with me.

We ordered some breakfast and got down to talking. He asked me several questions about my journey with kidney disease. Then, we started talking about dialysis in India. He knew very little about dialysis. However, he was very curious about every minor aspect. He was trying to understand how everything worked. He mentioned at one point that dialysis needed to be priced such that everyone is able to afford it. After all, how many people can spend that much money on the treatment of one individual in the family?

That night, I got an email from him asking some more questions. He also wanted to meet Jayaram Reddy, the technician from KIMS who used to come home for my dialysis. He also asked to be introduced to the sales guys at Fresenius, the company from which I had bought my dialysis machine. Over the next one month, we met many more times, continuing our discussion on the intricacies of dialysis and the dialysis ecosystem in India.

Vikram suggested that we needed to have two offerings—one would be the basic service, which would be priced in a manner that common people could afford it, and the second could be a premium offering that would have some frills and would be charged higher than the basic service. That seemed fine. There would be some people who would prefer getting special services at a higher price. Vikram also mentioned that he had signed up for a two-day workshop at the Indian School of Business (ISB) in Hyderabad. The focus of the workshop was to understand economically weak consumers.

During one of our meetings at a coffee shop in Apollo Hospitals in Hyderabad, after our interaction with Dr Somasekhar, one of the leading nephrologists in the city, Vikram officially asked me to join him in his venture on dialysis. He asked if I could invest Rs 20 lakh, which was the amount he was investing. Both of us would be 50 per cent owners in the company. I told him I would get back to him.

I had always wanted to do something in dialysis. Here was an opportunity that I would never get again. I felt this was my calling and had a good feeling about it. I had Rs 20 lakh in my bank. But that was about all I had. Effigent had wrecked finances. Whatever I had at that time was mostly the salary I drew at Grene. I discussed this with my parents. The Effigent experience had scared us. What if this turned out to be another Effigent? The similarities were striking. An entrepreneur with a dream, hoping to change the world. What if it turned out to be the same? I would lose all my money and my well-paying job. We decided against it.

I spoke to Vikram over the next few days and told him that I would love to be part of the venture but could not invest any money. I explained the reason behind it and the history of Effigent. Though this decision disappointed him, he understood completely. He was excited that I had agreed to be part of the venture. I also explained to him that since the company was still in its early days, I would not like to take the risk of abandoning a very well-paying job. I would work part-time for the new venture.

During the ISB workshop, they paired Vikram with a Sandeep Gudibanda for one of the activities. They hit it off well. Sandeep was a serial entrepreneur. He had been part of two start-ups in the past and had then joined ISB for his MBA. Sandeep was looking to join a start-up in healthcare as well. He wanted to be part of healthcare as an uncle of his, who was a doctor, had inspired him. He believed that one could make a greater impact by being in a healthcare provider company than by being a doctor. A doctor can only treat so many people per day. By being a healthcare provider, you might impact thousands of lives. Vikram asked Sandeep to join the venture we were working on. Sandeep agreed. Vikram also asked Sandeep to join the next meeting with me. I met Sandeep and was thrilled that another person had joined the team.

We started brainstorming on ideas for the name of the company and also started looking for places to set up the first dialysis centre. We had several email exchanges on the name. Each one of us came up with several names and the other two would weigh in. We came up with some whacky names as well during this exercise. We finalized NephroCare. Later, however, we realized that Fresenius, one of the world's largest dialysis machine manufacturers and service providers, had registered the brand NephroCare for use outside the US and we couldn't use it. We then switched to NephroPlus, while the company name would still be Nephrocare Health Services Pvt. Ltd. We registered the company on 18 December 2009. Vikram and his father were the two directors. We mentioned Vikram's parents' home in Hyderabad as our registered office.

Soon, we finalized a place as well. We set up the first centre in the MLA Colony area in Banjara Hills, Hyderabad. We saw several places before deciding on this one. It was part of a house, and we got to know later that it belonged to a friend of Vikram's father. We hired a company called 17D North to do the interiors for the centre. Apart from that, we also tasked them with coming up with a logo for the company.

What would be different about NephroPlus from the other dialysis centres that provided the same therapy? The machines were the same; the consumables were the same. We might carry out the protocols differently and more strictly. But clinically, there was nothing too different from what was already being offered.

When Vikram came across my blog, he saw something different from what he had encountered until then in his search about kidney disease and dialysis. He realized I was living a normal life. He saw I was proactive about my health. I was swimming every day and was working full-time. I took holidays at different locations from time to time. He realized that if he could get me to join as part of the founding team, it would give the company its USP. That would be the differentiator between us and the hordes of hospitals and providers offering dialysis services to thousands of dialysis patients.

The central theme of the company was going to be that dialysis patients could lead a normal life, and we were going to enable them to do that. We would look at everything from the patient's perspective. There were enough people looking at dialysis from a doctor's perspective and from a hospital's perspective. No one was thinking about the patient. We would do just that.

* * *

I think this formulation of the core belief of the company was very important and it was central to everything that followed. When I looked back and recalled what I had seen around me, there was no doubt left in my mind that this was what was needed in the Indian dialysis ecosystem. I had seen a lot of frustrated people, dejected because dialysis was not working for them. They were spending a whole lot but they were not experiencing any improvement in their quality of life.

I recall an incident. It was some time in December 1997. I was getting dialysis at Kamineni Hospital. There was an elderly patient next to my dialysis bed. He was very uncomfortable. There was a nurse continuously beside him, checking on his vitals. At one point, she panicked and called the senior nurse. The senior nurse rushed to the bed and saw that the old man was deteriorating. They called another doctor. He asked for the defibrillator to be brought. He took the two pads of the defibrillator and put it on the chest of the patient. The weak, fragile body of the patient literally quaked on the bed. One more time. And another. It looked as though the patient had been saved from death. He returned to stability. I do not know for how much more time though. I got done with my session and got out of there. I never saw that old man again.

Another man, who was getting treated at Kamineni, was around sixty years old. He was fine for the first few weeks. Then, he deteriorated gradually. After a point, I could see he was in pain. He hated every session. He was desperate for some relief. But how could he get relief? This cursed disease was a lifelong burden he had to carry. I think it was the needles that bothered him. He would scream with pain when the needles were inserted. He would loudly say, '*Jai Shree Ram*', repeatedly asking for divine help in relieving the pain. A week or so after that, I stopped seeing him. I asked a nurse what had happened to him. The nurse said softy, 'He expired.'

There was a devout Christian who got dialysis along with me at Kamineni. He was around forty years old. He was very regular with his dialysis sessions. I learnt that his kidney transplant had failed and that he was planning for a second transplant. After the second transplant, however, there were several complications. The transplant ICU in Kamineni was right next to the dialysis centre. So, you knew what was happening there. If not directly, you would get to know through the network. I saw a cardiologist take a big machine into the ICU. I met the patient's relative outside and asked him what was wrong. 'Only God must save him now,' he said. He passed away a few days later. When even a transplant cannot guarantee relief, what were we supposed to do?

Then, there was the young guy who walked into the KIMS dialysis unit one day. He was thoroughly breathless. He gasped with every breath. I could see the pain on his face. He collapsed into a chair. Jayaram asked him if he had brought the money. He reached into his pants pocket and took out a bunch of notes in various denominations. Jayaram shook his head and sent the money with a ward boy to bill the session. The guy couldn't afford dialysis. I have no idea how he got the money. But it couldn't have been easy. Jayaram quickly set up the machine and initiated his session. Later, I learnt that he could barely afford one session a week and collecting the money for the session was a struggle. Every week, he would be fully overloaded with fluid and would come in breathless to get a session that gave him his breath back. How much longer could this last though?

Then, there was this very cheerful guy who was on dialysis at KIMS, probably in his sixties. He would make everyone laugh with his jokes. One day, I overheard the nephrologist speaking to one of the technicians. Apparently, he had passed away a couple of days ago. It was not the fact that he had died that disturbed me. It was the manner in which he died that really upset me. He was staying with his daughter and son-in-law who looked after him really well. However, on that day, he was alone at home. Again, this was nothing new. He had been alone several times and could look after himself. But that day, he had a massive cardiac arrest. He fell to the floor and there were signs that he suffered for the last few minutes of his life, trying to reach out to his daughter. My gut wrenched when I heard this. Why not a sudden death, I thought? After all this suffering, when you had to go, why did you have to suffer some more?

This brings me to the fair, young guy at KIMS. Seven years younger than me, he was always bright and cheerful. He always had the mango juice-based drink, Maaza, during his dialysis sessions. I was very sad that he was diagnosed with end stage kidney disease (ESKD) at such a young age. If you get this kind of diagnosis when you are in the sunset of life, it can still be accepted with stoic calmness. But if you get this kind of sentence handed out to you in the prime of your youth, it can be quite a shock. This guy was fairly independent. He came to dialysis with his father's man Friday. I barely saw anyone from his family. He was on HD for a while, then switched to PD. One morning, I saw his picture in the obituary column of a newspaper. I rushed to my bedroom and cried. His death really shook me.

I had realized that this disease had only one way to end—with you. There was no cure, no relief. This was a lifelong disease. There was no guaranteed respite. When I was diagnosed, I was the only one of my age in the dialysis unit. However, I was now seeing several young people on dialysis. Many more lives were being destroyed. Many more dreams were being shattered. Nothing much was being done to improve the lives of those on dialysis. I often wondered why.

* * *

People think dialysis is the end of life. Almost everyone they know who is on dialysis, lead very dull, sick lives. Their entire life revolves around the dialysis session. Their routine is to simply go from bed to the dialysis centre and back to bed. I saw several such patients like the ones I have described earlier in my journey with kidney failure. A common thread I saw was misery. They were all tired of their lives. Life was an unbearable burden. To begin with, the treatment itself took a toll. You had to undergo four hours of dialysis once, twice or thrice a week, depending on different things. Those sessions would often be full of complications. You could have muscle cramps in your legs, feel dizzy, feel nauseated, etc. These were the simple challenges. Then, there were more serious complications, like a full-blown cardiac arrest or an epileptic fit. You could lose a lot of blood. Your blood could break up leading to other issues. An air bubble could enter the blood, which could also be fatal. Many people die during treatment because of other reasons as well.

And you had to pay for all this. Dialysis sessions costed between Rs 10,000 and Rs 30,000 per month then.

Once you leave the dialysis centre, your body and mind start playing a little game. The mind craves things that are bad for the body. It will want water. It will increase the desire for fluids of all kinds. The mind is a weird beast. Whatever is restricted, it craves. Doctors ask diabetics to restrict sugar. The diabetic will want anything sweet. Ask someone who is trying to lose weight to not have fried stuff. They will dream about fried food at night. Similarly, the minds of dialysis patients think about water. Even if you can get someone on dialysis to drink all the water in every single river in the world, they will still want some more water to drink.

Thirst is a primordial instinct of the human body. The body recognizes when it needs water, and within the mind arises the thought that the body needs water. This works well in people with healthy kidneys. However, this innate mechanism fails when someone is asked to restrict the amount of fluid they consume. Their mind craves water even when the body does not need it.

So, in dialysis patients, the problem is not the thirst in the body. The problem is in the mind.

They spend the time between dialysis sessions fighting this craving for water. Most dialysis patients drink more fluid than they are allowed. As a result, they come in for their dialysis sessions with a lot of excess fluid in their bodies. Often, this fluid accumulates in the lungs, causing severe breathlessness. Only dialysis can remove the fluid. The more non-compliant you've been with your fluid restriction, the more complications you are likely to experience in the dialysis session.

The situation is even more ironic in countries like India. Most people here have to bear their medical expenses themselves. The dialysis sessions are by themselves so frustrating that you don't feel like going for them. So, you end up trying to reduce your frequency. People who are prescribed thrice a week haemodialysis try to make do with sessions twice a week.

Governments in India have taken an interest in dialysis recently. Because of this, some patients get dialysis free of cost. Like many other government schemes, however, the implementation is quite flawed. Some governments pay only for ten sessions a month when, worldwide, the minimum frequency prescribed is three times a week. When patients get the benefit of being covered for their dialysis expenses, they still do not adhere to the prescribed regimen because of various other reasons. Some can't afford the travel costs to the dialysis centre. Others don't like the treatment itself and so try to skip a session from time to time.

During my initial years, when I was on haemodialysis, I found most dialysis centres looked like jails. They would be like dungeons with little lighting, smelling of chemicals and an almost continuous beeping sound from machines. No wonder patients hated to go to these centres. Billing counters would be on different floors than the centre. Patients would bill their session at the ground floor and then go to the centre to get dialysis, only to be told that they were due for some investigations or injections and would need to get that billed by going to the ground floor yet again. Why couldn't they do the billing at the dialysis unit itself? This would make it difficult for cash to be controlled, maybe. Was it really so difficult to institute a simple process to streamline dialysis billing?

When I compared myself with the typical dialysis patient, I found I was leading a very different life. My life was almost normal. I swam every morning, worked full-time, travelled, went for movies, ate out and hung out with friends. It was an almost normal life. Other than the dialysis sessions that I did at night, it was like anyone else's life.

What did I do differently?

The most important thing I did was to get more frequent, long-duration dialysis. I think this was a major factor that contributed to giving me a normal life. Why couldn't others do the same thing? I was not an ultra-rich guy. I came from a middle-class family. We managed somehow. We took a lot of loans. My parents' entire life savings were wiped out in the first few years of my diagnosis. But we somehow managed. Once I started working, things became even better. We slowly started paying back the loans. I started managing most of my medical expenses myself. This was a tremendous step in the journey towards normality. Being able to meet your own expenses with your income marks a major step in any dialysis patient's journey towards getting their life back. Until then, you depend on your family. Even though most families support dialysis patients (several do not), the feeling of being a burden is always there. So, becoming independent financially despite having a chronic condition is a huge psychological boost for one's morale.

So, was daily, nocturnal home haemodialysis the only way you could lead a normal life on dialysis? I don't think so. I was in touch with several people in India itself who were doing dialysis sessions in hospitals thrice a week and were leading pretty good lives. The difference between them and others was that they were getting good quality dialysis and that they had a positive bent of mind.

NephroPlus could not influence the adoption of daily nocturnal home haemodialysis in India. There was probably all of one patient getting it at that time—me. While there was no data on this, I guessed I had to be the only person. To be on this modality, you would definitely need support. Either your nephrologist would have to tell you about it or you would read about it on the Internet. In either case, you would have so many doubts that you could only get clarified online. There simply was no other way.

I was a member of the world's first and only support group for home haemodialysis, the one on Home Dialysis Central. Dori Schatell, who ran a not-for-profit in the US called Medical Education Institute (MEI), started this forum. Dori was a passionate advocate for patients with kidney disease. She had been in this space for over twenty years and ran several websites on various aspects of dialysis. I figured that if you needed some questions answered on home haemo, this was where it would be. During my initial years on home haemo, this was the only place I got support. During that time, I had seen no one with an Indian name or from India on this forum. So, I guessed that there might not be any other patient on daily nocturnal home haemodialysis in India. I might, of course, be wrong.

However, it was very unlikely that people were going to adopt this modality in droves. We would have to give them a better quality of life on the regular modality. There were two ways by which we would have had to address the problem. We would have to give them high quality dialysis itself, and we would need to make the experience more pleasant.

These would be the two fundamental things we had to focus on. Everything would flow from these two aspects. If we ensured a pleasant experience, they would not feel like missing sessions. Once they came for a session, we would make sure that the dialysis would be very efficient. This should, theoretically at least, translate to a better quality of life.

* * *

When we started designing our first centre, the main input we gave the interior designer was that the dialysis centre had to be bright and cheerful. We picked a bright but light green along with white and red for all our branding elements. The bright green represented the vitality and freshness of nature. We wanted our centres to be a source of joy and energy for our patients.

We also hired a few nurses, one of whom was Sara. Sara was a certified nurse who had an instinctive empathy for patients. She was an ideal healthcare worker who genuinely cared for her patients. She would take a lot of effort to bring a smile to their faces. I do not remember how we got to know of Sara. A lot of the elements of the NephroPlus culture stemmed from her approach to dealing with patients. During her tenure with us, she introduced several measures that would establish our culture of being patient-centric.

One day, when Vikram and I were sitting outside the cabin of a nephrologist waiting to meet him, Vikram said he was very uncomfortable introducing me as a 'patient' to the nephrologists and others we met. He said I didn't even look like a patient. Why should people call me a patient? He said we needed to think of another word to describe our patients. When our entire philosophy was that despite being on dialysis you could lead a normal life, why should we take away from that theme by using a word that brings a sick, bedridden person to mind? The entire team brainstormed. I do not remember who hit upon the idea of using the word 'guest'. It was either Vikram or Sara. Everyone loved that idea.

In India, we welcome guests like gods. That would add a perfect colour to our centres. We would treat guests and not patients! Guest care soon became the central theme of the company, with everyone adopting the term.

At this point, we felt we needed to get a senior dialysis technician on board. This person would help us understand the technical aspects of dialysis. The rest of us did not understand this at all. A thought occurred to me. Yellanna was a senior technician at Medwin Hospital and had dialysed me during my early days with kidney disease back in 1997. He also dialysed me when I got sessions at Medwin just after my PD infections, before I switched to home haemo. Being an experienced and knowledgeable dialysis technician, he managed the Medwin Dialysis Centre very well and had trained several technicians under him.

I suggested to Vikram that he might be our guy. We went over to Medwin and spoke to him. Yellanna remembered me. I thought Yellanna would not be willing to join us. To my surprise, he was very positive about it and agreed to join us in a few days.

Our first centre was to be ready for launch in the second week of March. We organized a small inauguration of the centre. It would have four dialysis machines and beds. We had some basic staff including a couple of technicians whom we had got from Medwin Hospital. This was to be a proof of concept. Would patients like our 'guest' experience? Would this take off at all?

On 14 March 2010, we launched the first NephroPlus centre. Our first guest, Taj Khan, who was earlier getting dialysis at Medwin Hospital but had moved to this centre as our first guest, inaugurated it. That theme—of having a guest inaugurate centres and be the centre of attraction for all events—continued forever.

We held a press conference to announce the inauguration of the centre. Vikram got introduced to a small-time PR agent who coordinated this and ensured that we got good coverage. While we all detest the media these days, it was important for people to get to know about us. A TV actress attended the event. At the end of the event, she made a rather blasphemous comment. 'I thank NephroPlus for inventing dialysis.' The local press carried that comment faithfully. This just goes to show the poor state of awareness among people.

The centre picked up slowly. However, everyone who came to the centre loved the concept. Standalone centres were new to the country. There had been a couple of companies that had tried and failed a few years ago. So, everyone was wary of how we would do. There were doubts about our survival. We got Dr Somasekhar, head of nephrology at Apollo Hospitals in Hyderabad to believe in us and send some of his patients to try our services. Vikram's uncle, who was a doctor himself, introduced him to us. Dr Somasekhar would also visit the centre at least once daily. He also liked the way the entire centre was designed.

I continued to work part-time for NephroPlus. During the day, I worked for Grene and, after work, went over to the centre at Banjara Hills and helped in whatever way I could. I was always available over call and email.

Despite all the good intentions, growth did not happen. The numbers just did not rise. The three of us met many nephrologists and requested them to try the centre. We would go to their consultation room and wait outside for hours, just to meet them and let them know about our dialysis centre. We were often given a curt response. 'Will see' was all we got, sometimes.

We tried hard to be different from the medical representatives who sat with us in the waiting areas outside the consultation rooms and were there to push pharmaceutical products.

Despite all our efforts, the numbers just did not grow to the next level. The staff were getting frustrated with the lack of growth.

We were all wondering what we could do next. What we did was something very counterintuitive. We decided to set up another centre. While this would test our ability to manage multiple centres when even one was not growing well, we believed that having multiple centres would improve our reputation among guests and nephrologists.

This time, we picked Secunderabad, the twin city of Hyderabad, where our first centre was located. We started scouting for locations. The same criteria as the first applied—space on rent with electricity and adequate water, in a place that was easy to find.

One weakness we discovered in our model was that the nephrologist did not have a stake in the success of the centre. They did not gain if the centre did well. They did not lose if the centre did not grow well.

So, for this centre, Vikram and Sandeep came up with a unique model to engage the nephrologist.

What we all understood clearly was that nephrologists were the ones who could advise dialysis patients to try us. Few patients would try a new provider on their own. While some providers employed nephrologists or paid them only per service, we made nephrologists co-owners of the centre.

The beauty of this idea was that the nephrologists had an ownership interest. If the centre did well, they would also benefit. If the centre did not do well, they would stand to lose. It was in everyone's best interests that the centre did well. This turned out to be a game changer in the way we worked with nephrologists, as we would learn much later.

In every such aspect, Vikram and Sandeep came up with out-of-the-box ideas that left me shaking my head wondering how they could think of that. One afternoon, while discussing the risk of cross-infections, I told Vikram that the Centre for Disease Control in the US had published a series of guidelines that advised against using common trolleys to ferry things needed to start and end a dialysis session. Vikram came up with the idea of having a small, plastic box that we would call the Zero Infection Point kit or ZIP kit. This box would have everything needed to do a dialysis treatment. In one stroke, we had a fantastic innovation. This wasn't a stupendous scientific innovation, but despite that, no one had thought about it until then.

That was the central problem in dialysis centres. Too little focus and too many patients resulted in almost no innovation. People continued to do the same things over and over again. The results had to be the same. While the guidelines recommended against the use of common trolleys, every single centre in the country continued to use these trolleys. Then people wondered why cross-infections with hepatitis C had become an epidemic in Indian dialysis centres.

For the second centre, Dr Somasekhar introduced us to a friend of his, Dr Krishnan, who was a nephrologist in the Secunderabad branch of Apollo Hospitals. This was the same nephrologist who had done my biopsy way back in 1997, which resulted in the diagnosis of atypical HUS. He remembered me and kept joking that he was the one who 'stabbed me in the back'. The biopsy procedure involved putting a thick needle in the back to pluck out kidney tissue, which is then analysed under the microscope to conclude which disease it is.

This centre was also going to be a standalone one like the first and was to be on the second floor of a commercial building. We hesitated to set up the centre on the second floor. There was a lift, of course. But what if there was an emergency? How would we transfer guests to an ambulance to rush them to a hospital? We decided we would take only stable guests and, in the rare case of an emergency occurring, we would have a wheelchair to transport the guest via the lift to the ground floor.

We got the health minister of the state, whom Sandeep knew through someone, to come and inaugurate the centre along with a guest. The night before the inauguration, the entire team, including Vikram and Sandeep, got the premises ready for the inauguration. I was unaware of what was happening. I got to know later that both of them sat down and scrubbed the floor to remove the plaster that was put to hold the tiles in place!

During the inauguration, we were explaining to the minister about dialysis, the importance of quality and how patients could lead normal lives on dialysis if the quality of the treatment was good. One of our Banjara Hills guests who had come for the inauguration exclaimed, 'Like NephroPlus!' This was the best testimonial we could have got for the work we were doing. While we may not have got the numbers yet, we were doing something right.

The second centre was inaugurated on 30 December 2010, about nine months after we launched the first centre. The attendance of the minister ensured much better press coverage.

We hoped that the new model would bring in guests. We hoped that having two centres would improve our reputation and we would not be seen only as a one-centre company. We had to continue our work of meeting nephrologists to see if their response was any different.

* * *

9

Differentiating Ourselves

'Oh, the comfort—
The inexpressible comfort of feeling
safe with a person,
Having neither to weigh thoughts,
Nor measure words—but pouring them
All right out—just as they are—'

—Dinah Maria Craik

In chronic conditions such as kidney failure, patients find others with the same problem immensely useful to get more holistic support in dealing with the disease. While doctors give medical advice and treat the disease, there are several other aspects to the disease that doctors may not consider clinically important but are bothersome to patients. This is where other patients come in. Based on prior experiences in dealing with issues commonly encountered, they offer advice which is invaluable in improving the quality of life.

Patient peer support is supposed to have originated in the late eighteenth century in a psychiatric hospital in France.[1] More recent reports from the 1960s, again in the area of mental health, have also been recorded. Patient peer support became mainstream in the 1980s when it expanded beyond mental health to other areas as well.

A few months after our first centre became operational, we came up with the idea of having a day that was dedicated to dialysis patients. There was a World Kidney Day. There were days for everything. Why not a World Dialysis Day? People typically observe these kinds of days to raise awareness for a particular disease or condition. So, we could organize an event for all dialysis patients and have talks by doctors, dieticians and so on. We could also make it fun by having some entertainment.

We went to meet Dr Somasekhar to discuss the idea. He was quite dismissive.

'You have one centre with five beds and you want to organize World Dialysis Day?'

We did not give up though. We started planning the event. That was the advantage of not having any baggage. You don't care about what people think and say. You come up with crazy ideas and you deliver on them.

We were to rent a hall in a centrally located, pleasant hotel. After looking at different options, we finalized on the Ramada Hotel Manohar, right next to the old airport in Begumpet in the heart of the city. We got an enormous hall that could accommodate about 500 people. The event was to be held on 6 February 2011.

We decided to name the event 'Aashayein' at some point. The name, we thought, should be something that resonated with Indians and *aashayein*, which meant 'hope', was apt. We also found a song called 'Aashayein' from a Bollywood film, which had a catchy tune and just the right message.

The event was to have educational talks by various specialists. I would talk on how to lead a normal life despite being on dialysis. A caregiver would give their perspective on living with a loved one on dialysis. A dietician would talk about the dialysis diet. A transplant surgeon would give a talk on how transplants are possible and who should opt for such procedures. A vascular surgeon would talk about various things patients can do to take care of their fistulas. We also planned a lot of entertainment like *antakshari*-type games. Our guests at the first centre would perform a skit. I wrote the script and practice sessions began.

We were also to have an elaborate lunch, as per the dialysis diet. Those not on dialysis would be served a simple meal of biryani and raita. When dialysis patients go for a wedding, they cannot eat most of what is served because of their diet restrictions. The food typically would have high sodium and potassium and could be quite dangerous for them. This event was for dialysis patients. So why not flip things around? An elaborate spread for them while the others got only a simple meal!

Another idea we hit upon was a 'Best Fistula' contest. A fistula is an 'access' for dialysis. It is created using a small surgical procedure. Over a long period, the veins of a fistula can start getting enlarged, forming large, scary-looking aneurysms. Most dialysis patients are embarrassed of their fistulae while we decided to have a contest for the best fistula. So, patients would come and flash their arms in front of a judge who would judge the fistula, and then we would call five finalists and have the vascular surgeon declare the winner.

The excitement started building in the run-up to the event. We started talking to doctors, whom we invited to speak on various topics. We also started contacting various dialysis centres and invited the patients there for the event. Some centres did not give us access to their patients. They probably looked at this as an exercise to try to 'poach' their patients. Who would do this without a selfish motive, they probably thought.

Our intentions were entirely honourable, though. We genuinely wanted to educate people that it was possible to lead a good life on dialysis. We never, not even for one moment, did this event intending to get patients to join us.

To overcome the potential negativity associated with this, we formed the Hyderabad Kidney Foundation, an informal trust that would be the organizer for this event. NephroPlus would be the chief sponsor. That trick worked, and we got better access to centres. One good thing that we realized from this episode was that people knew about NephroPlus and were worried that patients might move from their centre to ours. We were doing something right.

The day before the event dawned, we were all very excited. Adrenaline levels were probably higher than they might have been at a family wedding. During the night, as I got hooked to the machine, the team, including Vikram and Sandeep, were putting together the folders that would be given out to those attending the event. It had things like an agenda, lunch and tea coupons, a diet chart, a notepad and a pen.

On the morning of the event, we all gathered early at the venue. The weather was pleasant. Winter was wearing down in Hyderabad, so while the mornings were still a little bit chilly, by afternoon, it could get quite hot.

Worry tempered our excitement, though. Would people show up? The registration count had exceeded 500. How many would attend? Would all those who registered come? In that case, we were in for trouble. The hall couldn't accommodate that many. Would very few turn up eventually? Even bigger trouble. The event would be a flop.

At around 8.30 a.m., the first guest came with his wife. We were all thrilled. We made sure that the checking-in process would be as smooth as possible. Guests would go to the registration desk, collect their kit, go to the fistula contest desk to have their fistula examined and then take a seat in the hall. Over the next hour, more guests started coming. Almost all guests from our centre came. And others as well.

By around 10 a.m., the hall was almost full. The event would not be a flop.

We started the programme by inviting the senior-most nephrologist of the city, Dr Gopal Kishan, to light the lamp and inaugurate the Hyderabad Kidney Foundation. Dr Kishan spoke about the initiative that we had started in bringing support for dialysis patients of the city in glowing terms.

The event went off very well. Speeches made by the doctors and dieticians resonated very well with the audience. Everyone appreciated the food. The entertainment programme also went off very well. There was a performance by one of our patients, Hari Kishan, a famous mimicry artist, who did a stand-up comedy act where he made fun of dialysis patients, doctors, nurses and technicians. He was unsparing in his jokes. The audience could relate to them. His act was the highlight of the entire event.

When we wound up the programme at around 5 p.m., several patients came and thanked us. Many of them had tears in their eyes. They were experiencing something like this for the first time. By meeting several other dialysis patients, they could see, first-hand, how dialysis need not be the end of life.

This event was very important for the team as well. This gave them an opportunity to take care of dialysis patients in a setting other than the dialysis centre. It promoted team spirit as well. The team had to work together in a much larger environment. They also experienced what it meant to make a difference to the lives of those on dialysis. They enjoyed seeing the patients enjoying themselves.

To my mind, Aashayein was one of the most important initiatives NephroPlus ever undertook. The medical community was used to having lavish trips and cocktail dinners for doctors. Companies have such events for their teams. No one ever thought about the patients. The very patients because of whom we made a living. With this event, we brought the patient back to the centre stage. While we had already decided that they were the centre of our universe, this event sent a message to the entire dialysis community that NephroPlus had its heart in the right place.

* * *

Subba Rao* was a fifty-four-year-old farmer who stayed in Amistapur village, close to the town of Mahabubnagar, about 100 km from Hyderabad. Rao was diagnosed with kidney failure in 2008. A long-term diabetic, as happens often in rural India, he did not take his diabetes seriously and, in June 2008, collapsed while working in his fields. Luckily, his helpers were there to carry him to the local health centre where his blood sugar was found to be around 335 mg/dL. It should be below 140 mg/dL. The doctor there asked the helpers to take him to a hospital in Mahabubnagar. When he was taken to the Government General Hospital in Mahabubnagar, the doctors did a whole range of tests and he was diagnosed with end stage kidney failure. He had to get on to dialysis immediately.

This diagnosis came as a shock to Rao. He had two children, a son who was fifteen and a twenty-one-year-old daughter. His wife was illiterate, like him. The family was devastated by the news. There was no dialysis facility available in the entire Mahabubnagar district and they would have to go to a hospital in Hyderabad to get dialysis. Rao went along with his wife and daughter to the Nizam's Institute of Medical Sciences and got a slot for haemodialysis twice a week. He had to pay almost nothing as the treatment was covered by the state government for poor patients. However, the journey by train or bus to Hyderabad two times a week and back was torture for Rao and his family. One of the three would accompany him on the journey as he felt weak after the session and could not go back alone.

On one such occasion, Rao stood at the door of the speeding train, pondering on the mess his life had become. A thought occurred. If he jumped off, he could end it all. What was the point in continuing this life? As he was debating this, his wife who had accompanied him that day for dialysis, came looking for him and shouted out, asking him not to stand there as it was too risky. At once, his family came to mind. What would happen to them if he gave up? He returned to his seat, shaken from the experience.

The availability of healthcare facilities in rural India is a challenge. Many towns and villages do not even have more than a simple clinic with a registered medical practitioner (a substitute for a doctor) and basic medical facilities. Residents from these places have to travel to the nearest city to get anything complicated treated.

In the early 2000s, dialysis centres were mostly located in Tier 1 cities and only a few Tier 2 towns. Tier 3 locations almost never had one. Many patients in these villages would not even be diagnosed correctly if they were afflicted with kidney failure. They would die in a few weeks or months. Those lucky enough to get diagnosed would not have easy access to a dialysis centre. They would need to travel for hours, like Rao, to get to the closest one. Doing this twice or thrice a week, week after week, can be torturous for the patient and the family.

It was early March 2011. We had two centres. We had pulled off the biggest dialysis patient event in the history of the country. We believed that we had to be patient now. Things would improve, we told ourselves. We continued what we had to do. Ensuring good quality dialysis to our guests, taking good care of them, meeting nephrologists and convincing them to have their patients try us out.

And yet, after several weeks of doing this, things just did not move. There was only marginal growth. The three of us decided to meet to take stock and decide on the next steps. We did an 'offsite' in my house. My parents were travelling, so we had the house to ourselves. After a quick breakfast, we locked ourselves in a room and started from scratch. We had to figure out what was not working and a plan to fix that.

We talked a lot and could not find anything else that we could do apart from what we were already doing. Then the thought arose. Is a pure-play dialysis company truly doomed to fail? Would we also become like the chains that tried before us? Is India still not ready for this concept?

That was a possibility, we acknowledged.

The discussion veered towards broadening the scope. Could we offer a complete range of kidney-related services? Like maybe, dialysis access and other kidney-related treatments? We wondered what additional value could we offer.

And then, we started broadening the scope even more. Should we actually look at a full-fledged hospital offering all specialities? People were frustrated with the state of tertiary healthcare in the country as well.

This was where I became uncomfortable. Dialysis was close to my heart. Nephrology, I could still live with. But other specialities? Hmmm. Not so sure.

I paused the discussion and said that while I understood the challenges, I wouldn't be comfortable with such a broad scope of work in the company. I indicated that they could continue with this thread but I might not be part of it.

They understood. We left the discussion open. We did not reach any conclusion.

The next day, the three of us met in the office. No one mentioned a word of what had happened the previous day. We continued our work like nothing had happened.

A few days after that discussion, we got an inquiry from a hospital in Mahabubnagar. It was a hospital attached to a medical college called SVS Medical College. The word had spread. The press coverage, which we indulged in for business reasons— none of us hunkered for publicity—helped people become aware of our existence. Aashayein also contributed to this. How else would an obscure healthcare start-up, none of whose founding team members were doctors, get to be known by a tertiary care hospital?

This hospital was owned by an orthopaedic doctor who was also practising at Apollo Hospitals in Hyderabad. They invited us to come and set up a dialysis centre in their hospital. This was the next major challenge—running centres in multiple cities. The first two centres were only 10 km away. This was about ten times that distance. We were excited.

We did all the planning and build-out activity for the centre. This would be the first dialysis centre in that town. All patients, like Rao, were travelling 100 km two ways, twice or thrice a week to get dialysis.

Soon, it was inauguration day. We invited the local MLA. It so happened that the day of the inauguration was also the anniversary of my diagnosis with kidney disease. The sun was burning brightly that morning. Later, clouds eclipsed the sun and by the time of the inauguration, there was a bit of a drizzle as well. We had invited dialysis patients from the district as well. Many of them had come. Subba Rao came with his entire family. Their eyes became moist when they saw the centre. They couldn't believe that they could get dialysis in their own town and not have to travel far off any more. And the dialysis centre was much better than anything they had ever seen before. They came to us and explained their story. With a choking voice, Rao narrated how he was diagnosed and how he was going to Hyderabad twice a week to get dialysis. He also explained how his income had been reduced to a minuscule amount ever since he got on to dialysis. Now, with the centre just twenty minutes away, he believed he could finally get back to his fields in a serious manner and get on with life.

The three of us realized that this was it. Access and affordability were the two major problems with dialysis in India. This became our life's mission from then on. To bring dialysis within reach for the 'common man', both in terms of distance and price. Studies showed that only 15 per cent of those who needed dialysis in India were getting it. The rest were dying painfully.

The centre started soon after and within a few weeks, it was full. SVS Hospital got empanelled under the state of Andhra Pradesh's Rajiv Aarogyasri programme, which provided free dialysis for people who were below the poverty line. That way, patients did not pay for their healthcare needs. They were all covered for by the state. The cost of several procedures, including dialysis, were being borne by the state.

This was the future, I thought. There was simply no other option for India but state-sponsored healthcare. The millions of people who can barely afford basic food, shelter and clothing are unlikely to ever be able to afford decent healthcare. The only way this will happen is through the state.

Many people question the expenditure of the state's limited resources on chronic conditions like dialysis. Unless patients get a kidney transplant, this expense is lifelong. Most Indian dialysis patients are not productive. They are mostly at home, only venturing out for their dialysis sessions. In these circumstances, is it justified to spend so much on them? Isn't it more prudent to spend the money on reducing infant mortality, for example? Or labour deaths?

If you spend a sum of money on saving an infant, the return to society is much larger than spending money on someone's dialysis treatment. This is because the baby saved will grow up to be a productive citizen of society. On the other hand, the dialysis patient is being kept alive artificially and, unless they get a transplant, chances are that they will die in a few years. Even during the years that they are alive, chances are that they will not work. So, the spend on preventing infant mortality is a much better investment for the government.

However, there is a catch. The person who decides this prioritization is often a politician or bureaucrat. Politicians who run the country think of it from a completely different angle. For them, it is solely about winning the next election. Would they have a better chance of getting the vote of a dialysis patient and their family if they ensured free dialysis or if they instituted long-term programmes to prevent infant mortality? The former is what will most likely yield better results in the short term.

For dialysis patients, this works well. The Rajiv Aarogyasri programme showed the path for several other states to follow. Chief Minister Y.S. Rajasekhara Reddy had read the pulse of the people accurately. He knew that healthcare expenses had rendered several families penniless. There was a groundswell of support for the scheme when he launched it. Government funding of healthcare in India was here to stay.

* * *

Renowned management guru Peter Drucker has said, 'Culture eats strategy for breakfast.' However much we strategize, the culture of a company will be its route to success. We had to make sure that we developed a culture within the company that reflected our 'patient-centric' philosophy. We needed to make our guests feel like guests. The word 'guest' could not remain a hollow term.

If the three of us merely kept saying that we put the patient at the centre of everything we did, it would not be enough. We needed to live and breathe that idea. The three of us had to make sure that this manner of thinking transmitted to every teammate in the company. We would have to think differently and come up with ways in which we could do this. We did not have a rock star nephrologist as part of the team to ensure that people (other nephrologists and patients) flocked to us. It had to be the service.

This fresh perspective that we brought in to rethink the way we would set up dialysis centres and run them changed several things about the way people looked at dialysis in the country. People sat up and took notice. They could do things differently. We could solve problems that had been impacting patient lives for years. It did not have to be status quo forever.

There was something different about having a patient as co-founder of the company. This was an opportunity I did not want to let go of. This was my best chance to make an impact.

Among the few things that I wanted was a TV for every guest. Many dialysis centres in India would have only one TV for the entire dialysis centre of ten to twelve patients. I found that ridiculous. How could all patients be forced to watch the same channel?

I told Vikram and Sandeep that we needed to give each guest an individual TV with a satellite dish TV connection so that they could watch whatever they wished.

The average age of the dialysis patient was getting lower each passing year. We started seeing a lot of patients who were working. To enable them to work while they were on dialysis, I wanted to provide a Wi-Fi-enabled Internet connection.

All this would help make the session more tolerable.

I firmly believed that a kidney transplant offered the best quality of life to a dialysis patient. Vikram and Sandeep agreed when I explained this to them. When one of our guests would tell us that they were about to get a kidney transplant, while this was a business loss for us, we did not look at it that way. The entire unit would throw a 'send-off party', wishing them success in their upcoming surgery. This was one of the defining values of the company. Genuinely wanting the best for our guests.

On birthdays of our guests, we would bring in a cake and have them cut it in the centre. We would have their family come over and turn the affair into a small celebration.

All these aspects continued to be an important part of the company's culture. We had laid the foundation for what could be a company that changed the way dialysis was done. Our approach of keeping the patient at the centre of the universe was our best bet for success. That was the one thing that differentiated us from the others.

Recognizing this, over the next several years, we kept culture at the centre of everything we did.

* * *

We started NephroPlus with an initial investment from Vikram and his friends. Prabhakant Sinha, the founder of ZS Associates, a consulting company in the US for whom Vikram had worked in the past, had also invested. Since all three co-founders were from middle-class families, there was a limit to what our personal resources could do. This money could get us only so far. We needed serious capital. We realized this soon after the Mahabubnagar centre was started. We were running out of money. While we had set up and were running three centres by then, the company wasn't generating enough cash for us fast enough to be able to set up more centres.

One of the ways for a start-up to raise capital was through venture capital companies (VCs). These companies invested in several such early-stage companies expecting at least a few of them to become very successful and get them a good return on their overall fund investments. One problem with doing this was

VCs did not care about dialysis, about patients or about things like accessibility and affordability. They cared only about the return on their investment. As long as what the company did was legal and broadly within the framework of generally accepted ethical behaviour, they were all right with anything that got them a good return.

We were faced with a tough choice. We could either continue to grow very slowly, waiting till these centres generated enough cash for us to be able to invest in the next centre or ask VCs to invest in the company but make them shareholders. This would mean that they got a big say in the affairs of the company via the board of directors. VCs did not come cheap. Most founders dilute their stake in the company and hand over significant stakes to one or more such companies.

If we opted to grow only organically, there was no way we were going to make anything more than a marginal impact. Our dream of serving thousands of dialysis patients by setting up quality dialysis centres in their neighbourhood would remain only that—a dream. It was clear to us that VCs would be the only option. We started the process of raising money for the first round of investment into the company.

One thing I admire about Vikram is his networking skills. He already has contacts or has a way of digging out a connection anywhere. An MBA teaches you these things. Earlier, I never had much respect for MBA-holders. I always thought of them as those who could only talk well and not do much. They could make fancy plans, impressive presentations and could dress very well. However, when you looked a little below the surface, they would most likely be very hollow. Dhirubhai Ambani, the founder of the giant Reliance group of companies, had once said that MBA stood for '*Mane Badhu Aavde*' which means 'I know everything' in Gujarati!

Years spent with Vikram and Sandeep, both MBAs, changed that impression.

Vikram could find a common contact in almost any company. He found a common contact even in Alexion, the company that produced Soliris, the complement inhibitor that could enable me to have a successful kidney transplant. Nothing came out of it for different reasons. But Vikram used his vast network to get contacts among VCs as soon as we launched the Mahabubnagar centre.

Vikram and Sandeep prepared a business plan and a presentation about the company and our plans for growth. We started talking to different companies.

We travelled to Bengaluru to speak to Kalaari Capital. Rajesh Raju, a partner at Kalaari, was also a Chicago Booth alumnus like Vikram, and had been following our journey. He believed in us and was very keen on investing in the company. He invited us to come and present to their investment board. The three of us walked into the boardroom that had about twenty different people. We completed our presentation. During the question-and-answer session that followed, Vani Kola, one of the board members, grilled us quite hard. She somehow thought that it would be very difficult for us to partner with several hospitals and nephrologists. The meeting did not go well from there. We could sense that this was not going through.

Among other companies, we met with Bessemer Venture Partners (BVP). This, again, came from Vikram's amazing network. We met Vishal Gupta, a partner there. A few weeks later, we met Siddharth Nautiyal and Chitresh Modi in our East Marredpally centre. These guys were very classy. Siddharth asked us questions which demonstrated that he understood the business very well. They were interested in learning more. They made us feel at ease with their friendly demeanour.

The next day, they wanted to visit the Mahabubnagar centre. They reached there before us. We found them enjoying a dosa in the cafeteria that had a thatched roof and, where in the name of washing, they dipped a dirty plate in a bucket of reused water. Sandeep burst out laughing when he saw them there. These guys had humble cores. They could buy the entire hospital if they wished to and not even burp.

This could be an excellent partnership.

It became clear soon that BVP wanted to invest. We got down to discussing the terms of the investment. We would need some formal employment agreements for the three of us. Vikram did not have an agreement while both Sandeep and I had a simple one-page agreement. The new agreements for each of us would be several pages long.

The most important thing BVP would bring to the company, apart from funds, was structure. We could no longer run the company like a *kirana* store as Vikram kept reminding us. We would need to fill in several positions that would help us achieve that.

The most important thing that needed to be decided was what BVP would value the company at and how much money they would invest. This would also result in the share of the original investors getting diluted. Their share in the company in terms of percentage would go down. Because of the investment and the growth in the future, though, the value of the shares would go up.

This was the only way we could grow. This investment from BVP would be the first of more such rounds. None of us had family fortunes that could fund the expansion of the company. Each dialysis centre cost around Rs 1 to 1.5 crore. Our business plan talked about 100-plus centres over a period of five years. None of us had that kind of money.

Along with investments into the company, VCs and private equity (PE) players would also demand a say in major material affairs of the company. This was only natural. When someone put in so much money, they would expect decent returns for their investments. They were also answerable to the folks they got their money from. This meant that the investors would weigh in at the board level and, sometimes, even push hard in the direction they desired. Like every other entity, even investors come in various shades. Some are very intrusive. Others let founders do their thing, being available whenever needed. Most, at the very least, monitor progress at regular intervals.

Over the next few weeks, we finalized everything. We signed a term sheet with all key terms outlined. Legal experts worked on the final agreement drafts and within a few more weeks, all documents, including the shareholder agreement, were signed Share purchase agreement and employment agreements were created for the three of us. They transferred the money to the company account a few days after that. Vikram got an alert from the bank on his phone. It was an enormous amount. He forwarded that message to both of us. We had never seen that kind of money, ever.

To celebrate, the three of us went out to dinner at a restaurant called 'N'. We were grateful to each other for being part of this amazing journey. This was only the beginning.

We did a press conference to announce the funding. Almost all major newspapers covered it. The *Economic Times*, India's most reputed financial newspaper, carried the news on the front page of its national edition. That was huge! That single article alone would have registered in the minds of many people who mattered in the financial world.

Siddharth Nautiyal would sit on the board of NephroPlus. He had a stellar background. Having completed his BTech in computer science from Indian Institute of Technology Kanpur, he did his MBA from IIMA. Both these colleges were right at the top of their respective leagues. He had spent five years in McKinsey before joining BVP. He was a partner in their Mumbai office from where he invested in and worked with companies across various sectors, including e-commerce, clean energy, healthcare and hospitality.

Siddharth had this fantastic ability to guide us without being too intrusive. He brought a lot of value to the company by connecting us to various people, pushing us to bring more structure to the company and formalizing a lot of the processes that were happening in an ad hoc manner. Never did he make us feel he was interfering too much. It always seemed advisory. Chitresh Modi was his second-in-command, and he was also very good to us, helping us at every step of the journey.

One thing that gave BVP and other investors comfort was Vikram's leadership. Here was a guy with unquestionable ethics and an excellent understanding of business. Vikram always watched over the financials like a hawk. He understood investors did not give a damn about guests' outcomes or their smiles. For them, this was a financial transaction. He had to maintain the delicate balance between the vision of the company of enabling our guests to lead good lives and providing decent financial returns to investors.

Vikram did a fantastic job at maintaining this balance. In the Indian business landscape, it wasn't easy to find this combination—someone who was both ethical and successful. Having Vikram at the helm gave them the confidence that the company would do nothing unethical and would be mindful of investors' interests as well.

* * *

One summer morning in 2012, thirty-two-year-old Savitha Devi*, who was feeling a little breathless, had just settled into her dialysis session at one of the most reputed hospitals in Agra. The brutal summer meant her fluid weight gain was a little higher than usual.

As the hours went by, she started feeling better. She fell asleep, only to be woken up by the sound of the machine signalling the end of her dialysis session. A technician at the centre, Lalitha*, came to terminate her session. She started sending her blood back. As the blood was making its way into Savitha Devi's vein, another patient called out to Lalitha. The patient wanted Lalitha to call his wife, who was waiting in the hall outside. Lalitha explained that she was finishing up Savitha's session and would ask someone else to call his wife.

As Lalitha pondered and looked around to find someone who could fetch the patient's wife, from the corner of her eye she noticed that air had entered Savitha's needle and into her vein. Her heart started pounding. She panicked and clamped the line at once. Savitha was wondering why Lalitha was looking so tense. Lalitha asked her if she was feeling all right. Savitha nodded in the affirmative. Lalitha continued to complete the closing process. Within a minute, however, Savitha started coughing. Lalitha noticed her lips had turned blue. Going over to the end of the bed, she started cranking the lever there to place the bed in the Trendelenburg position so that Savitha's head would be lower than her body. She also asked Savitha to lie on her left side. 'Code Blue. Code Blue,' she shouted out. At once, all the staff ran towards Savitha's bed.

Savitha continued coughing. She was short of breath and suddenly had a stabbing pain in her chest. She was having a cardiac arrest. The hospital's emergency management team arrived in about ten minutes. The dialysis staff had put Savitha on oxygen support. Her body lay motionless by the time they shifted her to the ICU where she was declared dead because of an air embolism.

Dialysis sessions can be terminated in two ways—using air or by using saline (which is a solution of salt and water). In India, there is no standardization of protocols, including which closing method to use. Some centres use the air method, while others use saline. Patients sometimes prefer the air method, as they do not want even a single drop of fluid that is unnecessary to go into their body. However, with air closing, there is always the possibility of air entering the blood circuit if the person closing the dialysis session is not vigilant.

Lalitha was using the air method of closing, something she had done all her life as a dialysis technician. Everyone else in that centre also used the same method. They had only learnt that technique. But there had never been an incident like this before.

I learnt of it from the newspaper the next day. The hospital had fired Lalitha for negligence.

During my several years on dialysis, I had seen both methods of closing. I thought I had to make sure this never happened in NephroPlus. Similar to this, there were so many aspects of dialysis that could be done in multiple ways. Standardization was critical in a dialysis network that we were aspiring to be.

A lot of things changed once we got funded. We started expanding the central administration team. We hired an HR manager, someone to keep accounts, more people to manage operations and so on. The funds from BVP enabled us to do all this and ensure that the company started getting streamlined with different people doing different things rather than the three of us doing everything. By that time, I had quit my job at Grene and started working full-time with NephroPlus. The three of us had started drawing a salary as well. This salary was not anywhere close to market salaries, but, at least it was more than the 20,000-odd rupees each of us drew until then.

One of my family friends introduced us to a Dr Brian Pereira, a nephrologist of Indian origin, who had moved to the US decades ago and had done his MBA. He went on to become the CEO of a pharmaceutical company and later, a biotechnology company. Indian nephrologists held Brian in very high regard. What we had managed to achieve in a short amount of time impressed Brian.

We started talking to him about becoming a part of the company. We were thinking about having an independent director on the board, which comprised two people until then—Vikram and Siddharth from BVP. We would give him some stock options in the company in return. Brian agreed.

We held the second Aashayein event in February 2012. Brian agreed to speak at the event. The night before, we held a small meeting of select nephrologists from the city. Brian was to speak to them on a technical topic. When our team went to invite the nephrologists and mentioned that Brian would be speaking, some of them asked us if Brian was really going to speak or if we were simply using his name to attract attention!

Brian came, of course. He spoke very well and floored the audience, both at the nephrologists' meeting and the Aashayein event the next day. The Aashayein event went off very well. Attendance was higher than the previous edition. We had several doctors speak, and also had the 'Best Fistula' contest.

That same month, we started one more centre at Santoshnagar in Hyderabad. This was our fourth centre.

The next frontier was to go beyond one state. We started looking for opportunities in Bengaluru. Dr Sundar Sankar was a very senior nephrologist and the head of department at the famous Columbia Asia Hospitals. Reputed for kidney transplants, he used to follow my blog and had sent me an email in the past saying he always asked his students to read my blog to get a patient's perspective. He also mentioned that Dr J.C.M. Sastry was his teacher and that he had gone to see him during his last days in Hyderabad.

When Vikram, Sandeep and I had gone to Bengaluru for the meeting with Kalaari Capital for our first round of funding, I had called Dr Sundar and introduced him to Vikram. Vikram developed an excellent relationship with Dr Sundar over time. He recommended that we partner with his protégé, Dr Manoharan, for a centre in Bengaluru. Dr Manoharan suggested Koshy's Hospital in Bengaluru's Ramamurthynagar. Koshy's Hospital had a running dialysis centre, which already had some patients. Negotiations began and were finalized soon. We would run the centre end-to-end, just like the earlier centres in Mahabubnagar and Santoshnagar in Hyderabad. We also had an agreement with Dr Manoharan, who would oversee the centre as the medical director.

The centre posed new challenges for us. Running operations in an unfamiliar state was something new. Some regulations were different. We absorbed some staff from the old centre.

As we grew the network to four centres, we found it increasingly difficult to hire talent. Yellanna helped us hire some technicians and nurses. Beyond the first few centres, however, this search became problematic. We had one technician who was good at his work but was caught stealing some consumables. We fired him on the spot. Zero tolerance for corruption was going to be an important policy in the company.

Every technician we hired also did things their own way. To make sure that incidents like the air embolism in Agra never happened, we had to have standard protocols and all our staff had to be trained to follow them.

To solve this problem, we decided that the best way to do this would be to create our own talent pool. We decided to set up a dialysis training academy. We would call it Enpidia. Vikram came up with the name, a play on the acronym NPDA (for NephroPlus Dialysis Academy). We had an extra floor in the building that housed the second centre in Secunderabad. We did up a room there and created a classroom.

The next step would be hiring an instructor. This would be a very important position to fill. This instructor would train all our new staff about the right way to carry out dialysis. They would need to be good at the subject and also be ethical. They would need to believe in our guest-centric philosophy and the fact that with dialysis, people can lead normal lives. This was quite a tough ask.

Around that time, we came in contact with Phillip Varughese. Of Indian origin, Phillip was a facility administrator in a DaVita centre in the US. The Indian Society of Nephrology had organized their annual conference in Hyderabad that year, and Phillip had attended. He was associated with the Nephrology Nurses Association called NANT, which ran the BONENT certification programme for dialysis technicians and nurses. This was a reputed dialysis certification programme and carried a lot of weight in dialysis circles in the US.

We decided to tie up with NANT and offer courses leading up to the BONENT certification. Phillip put us in touch with NANT officials and we had to submit various documents to apply to be a certified academy offering the dialysis technician course that could enable people to take the BONENT exam. NANT approved our application and we became the only academy in India to be accepted for this programme.

I wondered if there were any BONENT certified technicians in India. I asked our HR manager to look for individuals with BONENT certifications on job portals. He found a tiny number of résumés. I interviewed a few of them and zeroed in on Venkatraman, who was working with Narayan Hrudalaya in Bengaluru. I pitched hard to him to quit his job and join as an instructor at the Enpidia Academy. Venkatraman joined us in April 2012.

The first batch of the academy started in the same month. We had asked the business development team to market the course among existing nurses and technicians and explain the importance of the BONENT programme. We got good traction quickly and enrolled our first batch, a mix of nurses and technicians.

Enpidia would lay the foundation for several important aspects of NephroPlus. The association with BONENT gave the technicians and nurses trained at the academy a solid foundation in dialysis and taught them how dialysis was to be done the right way. Venkatraman was a very energetic, ethical and knowledgeable person and did a fantastic job of training the students. He had excellent knowledge of concepts related to dialysis and had the benefit of working under stalwarts in the Indian nephrology ecosystem.

Venkatraman would make sure that our staff adopted standardized ways of doing things so that our guests were safe in our centres. We would design the protocols in such a way that mistakes would be minimal. Over the years, Venkatraman grew to take on the responsibility of being the country head of clinical quality for the company.

We would also adopt a higher goal with dialysis. Dialysis can be done in two ways. One simply prolongs life. The other helps the patient thrive. Unfortunately, in India, most dialysis simply prolongs life. Very few centres provided dialysis that enabled patients to thrive. At Enpidia, we were committed to the latter. We wanted every single guest at NephroPlus to live a full life.

Apart from the theoretical and practical aspects of dialysis, we would also teach our students how to interact with guests pleasantly. Our guests were undergoing tremendous difficulty with this disease. Not wanting to treat just the physical aspects of the disease, we were very mindful that this was a psychological condition as well. We needed to make our guests feel good when they came to the centre. We needed to ensure that the centre became—to use a cliché—a home away from home.

* * *

10

Brick by Brick

'Success will surely come with time and labour,
If we our aims will carry far and high,
For we can win the plaudits of our neighbour,
And reach the goal by perseverance by and by.'
—Bernhardt Paul Holst

Fifty-three-year-old Radheshyam Singh*, a resident of Rohtak, Haryana was a dialysis patient at a hospital with four dialysis machines and a modest set-up. Diagnosed with kidney disease in 2011, he used to get dialysis twice a week using a temporary catheter, which was inserted in a vein close to the neck. The catheter would work for a few weeks and then get infected. The doctor would then insert a new catheter. This cycle kept repeating.

Getting dialysis using a catheter is not ideal. Repeated infections put a lot of strain on the body. Singh's doctor had advised him to get an arteriovenous fistula (AVF) by surgery. Singh could not gather the money for an AVF surgery, which would cost about Rs 20,000.

A catheter cost him Rs 2500 and would last him a couple of months. It worked out better as Singh relied on the monthly assistance he got from his brother, who was funding his medical expenses. He could not get the money needed for an AVF surgery, even if this made more financial sense in the long term.

Clinically, AVFs are the best option among all access types for dialysis. Less likely to get infected as they are beneath the skin, AVFs can last decades compared to catheters such as the one Singh was using, which don't last beyond a few weeks. Dialysis quality using catheters is often not as good as that with an AVF.

A lot of patients in north India got dialysis using catheters. Lack of awareness and paucity of funds for an AVF surgery were the most important reasons.

Towards the end of 2012, we had eight centres. Six were in the state of (then united) Andhra Pradesh and two were in Bengaluru in Karnataka. The next logical step was to expand to the north. I do not remember how we were put in touch with Pushpanjali Hospital in Agra. It had a very poor-looking dialysis centre. The hospital wanted to outsource to us. We soon finalized the commercials. Mayank Agarwal, the owner, was a young and shrewd businessman. He had multiple businesses, many of them being handed down from his father, V.D. Agarwal.

We renovated the centre. Bright, cheerful interiors replaced the depressing, dark centre. We installed new machines and added staff. We launched operations on the first day of 2013. The guests, the staff and the hospital partner were all thrilled with the way things had changed. Mayank Agarwal would bring people just to show them the dialysis centre.

The contrast in culture between north and south India was quite stark. People in Agra were much more boisterous and aggressive. They would make many unreasonable demands and expect you to accommodate them. One guest's son in the Agra centre insisted we allow him in the centre at all times while we had a strict 'no attendants' policy in all our centres. No amount of explaining or flashing the rule book would help. The language was also crude and offensive. We encountered such people everywhere. Our staff, the partners, vendors we dealt with—most people were like that.

Several theories have been put forth to explain the aggressive behaviour of north Indians as opposed to the comparatively docile behaviour of those who live to the south of the Vindhya mountains of India. India has seen many invasions from outside. All invasions almost always were from the north or the north-west. Because of this, the people in that area have become accustomed to fighting for their rights and dignity. Few invaders ventured south and Indians beyond the Vindhyas were spared this misfortune.

How true this explanation is, I do not know. What I do know is that people in the north, especially in the Hindi belt of Delhi, Haryana and Uttar Pradesh, have a more aggressive demeanour than their southern counterparts. But, NephroPlus was here to stay.

A few months after we started the Agra centre, we got to know about a hospital in Rohtak through a reputed nephrologist at Gangaram Hospital, Delhi, Dr A.K. Bhalla. We finalized terms and started operations there as well.

Radheshyam Singh got to know about the centre and moved there. Our team counselled him about the risks of getting long-term dialysis with a catheter. Led by Surender, an experienced dialysis technician who joined us when we launched the centre, the team there was committed to improving the quality of our guests' lives. He convinced Singh's brother to pay for the surgery after explaining how much he would save in the future.

In a few days, Singh got his AVF surgery and within a few more weeks, he switched to dialysis using the AVF. The quality of dialysis possible was much better. Apart from the change in access, the dialysis parameters, which our team closely monitored, also helped. In a couple of months, Singh, who was earlier brought in a wheelchair from the main hospital gate, drove himself to the centre on a motorcycle for dialysis.

By this time, we also hired our first management team member. Rohit Narula was Sandeep's classmate at ISB and joined as head of operations. Rohit had completed his marine engineering and worked in the merchant navy for a few years before joining ISB for his MBA.

We also expanded our central administrative team. We got people in human resources, finance, MIS and business development, and more people in operations as well.

One thing we had realized was that India was not ready for standalone centres. While a few of our centres were, we felt that centres inside hospitals were the way to go given the current circumstances in India. Standalone centres provide a feeling of not going to a hospital for something as routine as dialysis. However, because of the higher rate of complications among Indian patients compared to those in developed countries and because of the lower average frequency of dialysis, patients feel more comfortable when they are inside a hospital. They feel that should something happen to them while on dialysis, at least there is an ICU and an emergency team to take care of them.

By mid-2013, we had fourteen centres. Until then, we had only partnered with smaller hospitals. We did not have any centre in a reputed, famous hospital. That was our next goal.

Max Healthcare is one of India's largest and most reputed hospital chains. Currently operating in sixteen locations, the company was founded in 2000 by Analjit Singh, the youngest son of Bhaimohan Singh, owner of Ranbaxy Labs, one of India's most reputed pharmaceutical companies.

Analjit Singh sat on the board of ISB. Sandeep knew the dean of ISB, Ajit Rangnekar, very well. This was a great opportunity for us to try and get entry into a famous hospital chain.

Rangnekar put us in touch with the Max team through Singh.

We pitched NephroPlus to them and after a lot of back and forth, the Max team signed a contract with us. All dialysis centres that Max outsourced for the period of the contract would be to NephroPlus and no one else. They would hand over the dialysis centres of two hospitals—the ones in Patparganj, Delhi and the one in Dehradun—to us to operate.

This was huge. By itself, this contract was a massive win because of the potential opportunity. NephroPlus could, in the future, run the dialysis centres of all hospitals of the chain. To top it all, this was Max Hospitals, one of the top brands in the country.

There were several things that were different about this contract, though.

We would not have any financial arrangement with the nephrologists. Max would continue to employ them, and we would only pay Max. There wasn't going to be any major branding of NephroPlus inside the centre. We could put only a coy NephroPlus logo at the main entrance of the centre. Further, the hospital would continue to do the billing of all the sessions and would pay NephroPlus at the end of the month.

All these changes were quite major compared to what we were used to at all our centres. However, we had to compromise on these things to bag a contract as massive as Max Hospitals.

We also realized that this was a turning point for the company. This meant that the big boys of Indian healthcare had now accepted us. We were no longer only a standalone and minor player in the dialysis ecosystem in India. We had finally arrived.

* * *

Around the same time as the discussions with Max Hospitals were going on, I got a call from Sandeep one day requesting me to be present at our East Marredpally centre. This was our showcase centre where we brought anyone who wanted to see our centres and meet us. A team from a potential hospital partner, Jehangir Hospital in Pune, was visiting and since he and Vikram were both not available, they wanted me to handle that meeting. I was not at all used to doing business development. My skills were restricted to offering ninety-five rupees if asked for a hundred rupees. I agreed reluctantly. One of our senior BD managers was going to accompany me.

I met the senior management of Jehangir Hospital and talked them through my journey and NephroPlus. They seemed to be very affable people, genuinely interested in us. The discussions proceeded rather quickly and in September 2013, just around the time when the Patparganj Max Hospital centre started, we announced the inauguration date for the Pune centre.

I flew down for the launch along with Vikram. The owner of the hospital, Cowasji Jehangir, had an illustrious lineage. His ancestor, Sir Cowasji Jehangir, had been conferred with a title in the baronetage of the UK in 1908. By a special act of the legislative council of India in 1911, they decided that all future heirs would assume the same name and title. Cowasji Jehangir, who was running the hospital, was fourth in line. He also takes the title of baronet, so people refer to him as Cowasji Jehangir Bt.

Mr Jehangir had organized a cocktails-and-dinner party the previous evening in our honour. We interacted with the board members, doctors and administrators of the hospital. There was a very warm vibe about the evening.

One doctor said something that was very striking: 'One thing that is unique about this hospital is that they do not give us targets for things like labs and procedures.' This was a refreshing change from the blatant commercialization that we had seen in the three years we had been in healthcare.

It is indeed sad that this should be something unique about a hospital. Shouldn't this be the norm? Why should doctors be given targets for investigations and procedures? Are they salespersons? Are products being sold? Aren't we dealing with human lives here?

The next morning, we inaugurated the centre and followed it up with a press conference. Mr Jehangir made a very significant point during his address to the press: 'One can spend hours and hours drafting legal agreements, making sure every clause is fine. However, when both parties have similar values and can trust each other, all that effort is much less important.' Truer words hadn't been spoken.

Our relationship with Jehangir Hospital turned out to be one of the finest among all our hospital-partner relationships. One of the management team members would always make it a point to fly down for their annual foundation day in February.

The west zone turned out to be one of the best to deal with in terms of people.

One of our biggest 'catches' was soon to come, though.

Dr Umesh Khanna was a reputed nephrologist from Mumbai. We had read his seminal paper, 'The Economics of Dialysis in India' published in the *Indian Journal of Nephrology* in January 2009[1] which was almost like the gospel for anyone looking to do some work in dialysis in the country. When he visited our stall that had been put up in the exhibition area of the annual conference of the Indian Society of Nephrology, Vikram and I had a fanboy-like moment when he introduced himself.

Sandeep started talking to him about outsourcing his centre in Borivali in Mumbai. The centre was very cramped. The beds ran along the walls of multiple rooms, many of them like corridors. You couldn't tell which patient was connected to which machine unless you followed the blood line to the machine. The centre itself was split into multiple sections, some even on different floors in another building. This was not easy to manage. The building also housed a restaurant causing pests, including rats, to visit the centre now and then. They stored the RO water in small tanks placed on the parapet that were connected to each other through pipes. This was a centre that was different from what we had done so far. Yet, the one thing that was attractive about the centre was the nephrologist, Dr Umesh Khanna. Because of that name, the centre was teeming with patients.

Dr Khanna was a tough negotiator. He knew his worth and was determined to extract the full value. Negotiations went on for months. Sandeep led this from our side. There were several instances where we would be close to agreeing, but suddenly, something new would crop up and we would be back to the discussion table. What made this deal complicated was that the hospital partner and the nephrologist partner were the same person. In regular circumstances, we dealt with two different parties for these two aspects. Here, both were the same.

Finally, Vikram stepped in. He flew down to Mumbai. After several hours of protracted discussions, the two men arrived at an agreement at Dr Khanna's home. Vikram sent us a picture of them shaking hands after signing the contract. I almost jumped up with excitement while connected to my dialysis machine late at night.

The next day, the Mumbai nephrologist community was agog with excitement. WhatsApp messages in nephrology circles proclaimed, 'NephroPlus nets huge catch, the biggest name in nephrology from Mumbai suburbs.'

Dr Khanna was also going to be on our scientific advisory board, something that was included in the entire package with no additional compensation.

We had indeed come a long way. From reading his article in a journal to meeting him for the first time at the conference and then finally signing him up as our partner, we had indeed done pretty well for ourselves.

I think one of the most important reasons for our success was the professional way in which we ran the company. All collections and payments were official. There was no question of any black money. We kept our word, always. We were straightforward people. This had helped to build an impeccable reputation among the nephrology community in India. When people did not have to fret over basics, they only had to be concerned about their work and not worry about whether we were cheating them or forging papers. This was an immense advantage in those times.

* * *

The western region, especially Mumbai, became home to many dialysis centres, run by various trusts. They provided dialysis sessions to those who could not afford treatment in for-profit hospitals and dialysis centres. Some other parts of the country have also seen similar trust-run dialysis centres come up.

Even for a middle-class family, the monthly recurring expense of about Rs 20,000 can be a strain on the household budget. The poor can't even think of this. In these circumstances, these trust-run centres are lifesavers. Without these centres, these patients would get dialysis for a few months or years, drain their family's savings and then, die.

The trouble with kidney disease, as Inderchand Jain—one of the trustees of the Bhagwan Mahavir Jain Relief Foundation Trust based out of Hyderabad and running several such dialysis centres—told me one day is that it is a continuous, lifelong expense. Unlike a heart condition that can be treated with a bypass surgery or cancer, for which you have a few months of rigorous treatment and then you either die or are in remission, dialysis patients have no respite from this treatment and the associated expense.

Manubhai Turakhia*, a Gujarati businessman who was born and raised in Mumbai and stayed in the Ghatkopar suburb of the city, was a man of limited means. He was earning just enough to provide for his family—wife, son and daughter. He traded in mobile phone parts, which he got in bulk from various agents who, in turn, sourced them from various manufacturers in China and Taiwan, and sold them to small-time mobile service centres. He had established himself over the years, but the margins kept shrinking, which meant that his income stayed almost the same.

A storm came into Manubhai's life when he was diagnosed with kidney failure in December 2008. A long-term diabetic, he had not kept his blood sugar under control and this resulted in his kidneys being damaged slowly over the years, without him realizing the fact. One evening, he noticed his feet were swollen. He had been feeling more tired than usual during the day. On his wife's insistence, he visited the neighbourhood doctor who got some tests done which revealed kidney failure. The doctor asked him to consult a nephrologist who told him about the extent of the damage.

That entire night, Manubhai couldn't sleep. Thoughts about what would happen to him, how his family would survive if he died, how he would arrange the money for the treatment, etc., bothered him.

He then heard about a dialysis centre run by a charitable trust. The trust was involved in several other charitable activities, and they had set up this centre a few years ago. They charged patients a token amount of one rupee per dialysis session. This was a boon to the about 200 patients that were getting dialysis there.

Manubhai got to know about the centre from the nephrologist who visited the centre daily. He was thrilled to know that he could get dialysis almost free of cost there. He registered with the centre and started dialysis in a few days.

Some people argue that dialysis centres run by charitable trusts do not offer good quality dialysis and are only prolonging lives by a few months or years. They say professionals do not manage these centres and have little oversight, resulting in the technicians running the centres as they like.

While this may be true sometimes, several such centres are run very well and have committed and passionate teams that have patients' best interests at heart. It all depends on the leadership. If the people driving the operations of the centre are interested in providing quality dialysis and making their patients lead good lives rather than simply adding months with no improvement to the quality of life, then the entire system falls into place and they achieve the result. If the management adopts an approach where they oversee operations superficially leaving everything to the technicians, then the centre degenerates into a factory-like system where dialysis is done with little improvement to the quality of life.

Aren't for-profit dialysis centres also like that? Several such centres are managed well and are committed to improving outcomes for patients. But several others are managed poorly and patients go there because there aren't any better options and have a poor quality of life. Merely being for-profit does not guarantee good clinical outcomes.

When someone gets diagnosed with kidney failure and is told that they would need to spend Rs 20,000–30,000 a month to stay alive, it can be devastating for the entire family. These centres become the only hope for such patients who cannot afford this massive expense month after month. Even assuming that they go to one of the poorly managed centres, they have the satisfaction of not giving up. They feel they have done something about the disease. Lack of money did not cause them to just waste away and die. Their life may be prolonged, in the worst case, by only a few months or years. That is better than dying because they did not get any dialysis at all.

If they go to a well-managed dialysis centre run by a charity, their life can almost return to normal. I know of several people who have returned to work full-time after getting dialysis in charity centres. The joy of getting your life back without draining the family's limited resources in these circumstances is unimaginable.

If some wealthy people have the resources to give these people hope, why should anyone question them? They get some fame. True. What is the harm? They have their own or their parents' names printed on the machines and walls of the centre. What is the problem with that? The centre is saving lives. Patients and their families are getting hope. The money spent is giving hundreds of families moments of togetherness, which would have been impossible otherwise.

Manubhai Turakhia got his life back. He resumed his work, albeit less strenuously. As of the time of writing this, he is doing very well. His family couldn't be happier. Manubhai has also saved small amounts in various financial instruments so that whenever he passes away, his family will have something to fall back on. The charity centre gave him enough time to take care of this. He is also grateful to the trust for providing him and scores of other patients the opportunity to get dialysis. Kidney disease was a death sentence that came to all of them suddenly. The trust's dialysis centre saved him from death and his family from ruin and uncertainty.

* * *

By early 2014, we had about twenty centres. We needed more people at the top to manage the growing network. We were also adding centres at a rapid pace. Almost every month, one or two centres got added. Rohit Narula was looking after operations, which was becoming challenging. He had lieutenants to help him, but they had limited capabilities. We also had some junior people managing things like finance, inventory and so on. I was looking after clinical aspects and all guest engagement activities and related issues. I was also looking after IT. Sandeep focused on business development. Vikram oversaw the entire system.

We got Vaibhav Joshi, a chartered accountant (CA) who had worked for a multi-store retail company in the past, as finance controller. We also hired a young IIT graduate with experience in consulting, Sohil Bhagat, as executive assistant to the CEO. Vikram was getting stretched with various activities and could do with some help on that front. Over time, we had some changes in the operations team as well. Rohit Narula left. Rahul Khandelwal joined and left within a year. Sohil and I took over operations. We managed for about fifteen months after which Ravi Dikshit, an MBA with experience in distributed operations in lifestyle clinics and salons, joined us and took over operations.

We kept witnessing attrition at the managerial level as well. I felt a little unnerved by this. I could make peace with attrition among the dialysis centre staff. These people would switch to a company offering only 3–4 per cent more as well. However, at the management level, it was surprising. We also asked some to leave because of non-performance or a lack of synchronization with our values.

Realizing that we would need more money to fund growth, we went in for another round of funding. This was the Series B round. We started the process. We prepared all the material needed for the fundraise—the pitch deck, the business plan and so on. Vikram also got in touch with several contacts and reached out to a few PE companies who might be interested. We started having meetings.

We learnt that International Finance Corporation (IFC), which was the investment arm of the World Bank, was interested in us. Pravan Malhotra, the Indian partner of IFC, and his team came to Hyderabad, and we met them at ITC Kakatiya Hotel. We ran through the presentation and our story. The meeting went off very well. While IFC was a PE, their investments had to have an 'impact' angle. Traditional PEs wouldn't care about what the company did, provided it was not illegal and had a good chance of making multiple times the money invested. IFC was different.

When we got done with the meeting, I remembered making a comment to the rest of the folks who attended from our side: 'This is going to go through.'

The due diligence process started. It was multipronged. It was much more thorough compared to Series A. I guess this was because the size of the company had grown and also because of the very nature of IFC.

We had several people from various internal teams within their organization visit some centres. One of their managers, who visited one of the centres we had set up through a public private partnership (PPP) model made the most interesting comment. The Employees' State Insurance Corporation had outsourced a dialysis centre that they were running to us. I was present during that visit. He remarked that no one could tell that it was a PPP centre. He wondered how we could maintain such outstanding quality even for a PPP centre.

Another person, an American, who visited another centre, commented that if his mother were to ever get on to dialysis, he would like her to get dialysis at our centres. This was a tremendous compliment coming from someone who was used to top-notch healthcare services back home.

After an exhaustive due diligence process, IFC made us an excellent offer. My prophecy turned out to be true. We signed the term sheet and closed the funding round in about six months, which was a record of sorts. IFC had the reputation of being a very slow-moving organization, almost government-like. They usually took several quarters to complete the investment process.

I do not know what caused them to move so fast. Was it the comfort they had with our story or our above-board ethics? Was it Vikram's reputation among investment circles? Or was it some internal deadline that they had to meet around impact investments? We might never know the answer to that question.

We were thrilled that IFC came on board. Having an impact-oriented investor was a wonderful thing for a company like ours. IFC also brought in discipline on overall compliance. From then on, having compliance in place became a prerequisite for any new deal to be signed.

The good thing about IFC is that they have several initiatives, such as an Innovators Forum, where early-stage companies can collaborate or carry out research studies on various topics using their funds. The best part about getting an investment from IFC was that it added a lot of weight to our reputation among investment circles. It was, after all, an offshoot of the World Bank. In effect, the World Bank had invested in us.

* * *

Growing a company from scratch to this size requires some solid processes. It needs all management teammates and even their direct reports to be in sync with each other. We instituted several such processes that helped streamline communication.

A lot of the credit for these processes must go to Vikram. He brought with him years of experience in working with teams at the highest level. He also had a sharp intellect and wonderful insights into what would and would not work for teams such as ours.

From the early days of the company, when only the three of us were part of the management team, we had a daily morning call.

We would dial into a conference bridge and have a quick catch-up with each of us outlining the plan for the day and discussing any issues that needed attention. This was an excellent way to ensure that the three of us knew what the others were up to. The calls continued for several years.

It was a pain for most people, though. While getting ready for work, finishing one's morning ablutions and whatever else was part of the routine, at a designated time, they had to leave everything else and join the call. For many people, because of sleeping late and getting up late, mornings are very rushed and the morning scrum turned out to be a problem.

However, the benefits of doing it were immense. Most people appreciated that. So, while it was a difficult thing to do, people did it.

At one point, people started ignoring it and would skip it. Vikram instituted a financial penalty for those who missed these calls. To reduce the pain, we decided that all penalty money would go to the Aashayein Kidney Foundation (AKF), a trust we had formed to help fund treatments of guests who could not pay for them. We started off by funding small things like blood tests, injections and minor surgeries, such as those for a dialysis access.

The money that the teammates were paying was going to a good cause and not to the company. This reduced the pinch somewhat. We expanded this system of penalties being directed to AKF for everything else in the company as well. If people did not respond to important data requests in time or did something that was not in line with company policies, we imposed a penalty that would go to AKF. People started calling these penalties 'AKF penalties'. I was uncomfortable with that because I was afraid that people would start looking at AKF negatively.

Daily reports was another practice that we implemented. Again, thanks to Vikram. Every teammate above the centre manager in the hierarchy sent a daily report to their immediate supervisor and copied the person at another level up the hierarchy. Management team members sent it to all their counterparts. To Vikram's credit, even he, despite being the CEO, was sending daily reports to the management team. A penalty was imposed if people did not send their report by noon the next day.

Again, this was a practice people hated. Apart from the pain of keeping track of what one did the entire day and remembering it towards the end of the day or the next morning, some people believed that daily reports were necessary only if you didn't trust your team. That is a fair point. However, a daily report gave the manager a sense of what their teammates were doing. We wanted to ensure a transparent environment where each team member would know what other functions were working on. It was a great way for them to keep in touch with activities happening in their team and also understand what was going on at the macro level in other functions.

People also hated the fact that we penalized them for not sending their daily reports on time.

At one point, we introduced a Monday morning meeting where all management team members would get together in the conference room and go over high-level initiatives and issues that needed a group discussion. A few months later, we felt that this was too frequent. It was replaced with a monthly business review (MBR). We typically held it during the middle of the month. The finance and strategy teams would prepare a presentation which would summarize the financial status of the company, such as the profit and loss (P&L) statement of the preceding month, trends, receivables and so on. We found this process to be very useful and did it continuously.

The board of directors plays a very important role in the company. Legally, the board is responsible for everything that happens in the company. In the beginning, the board comprised

Vikram and his father. When BVP invested in the company, Siddharth Nautiyal replaced Vikram's father. Siddharth added a lot of value to the company. Never getting involved in the day-to-day running of the company, he gave us some precious tips and advice on high-level strategy, etc.

Series B saw Pravan Malhotra get added to the board. Things continued similarly. The board never got involved in day-to-day activities, and we sent them regular updates on financials and other major happenings.

We also worked on a scientific advisory board. Work on this happened around the same time as Series B. We got in touch with Dr Vivekanand Jha who was the executive director of a prestigious not-for-profit institute called the George Institute for Public Health and a professor of nephrology at the University of Oxford. Dr Jha was from Ranchi in east India and had completed his MBBS from Patna Medical College. He did a post-graduation in medicine and nephrology from the reputed Postgraduate Institute of Medical Education and Research (PGI), Chandigarh.

Dr Jha is the most reputed academic nephrologist in the country. He held various positions in several bodies such as the International Society of Nephrology (president), Asia Pacific Society of Nephrology (president) and Indian Society of Nephrology (various posts). He was among the top 1 per cent of quoted authors in the world in nephrology.

Dr Jha had such a distinguished record that we were not even sure he would work with us. On a trip to Delhi, Vikram got an appointment and went over to meet him at his office. He found Dr Jha to be an affable, honest and ethical person with a deep interest in research. He had his own research lab in PGI, Chandigarh. The vast amount of clinical data that we had collected intrigued Dr Jha.

From around 2013, we had invested in the development of an IT backbone for our company called the back office portal or BO portal. Apart from things like billing and inventory, we captured all the clinical data of our guests on this portal. Dr Jha was very interested in this data.

There is a background to this.

Very little clinical data exists from developing countries like India. Most research that is published has data from developed countries like the US and Europe. So, when he came to know that we had clinical data of thousands of dialysis patients from India, he was excited. We asked him if he could be our medical adviser. We discussed the terms and signed the agreement quickly.

We constituted the scientific advisory board (SAB) and requested Dr Jha to chair the board. He agreed. Dr Umesh Khanna and Dr Rajasekhara Chakravarthi, a reputed nephrologist from Hyderabad (whom I eventually moved to for my own clinical care), would also be part of this board. This board would be responsible for all clinical protocols and all clinical aspects at a high level. We formalized an annual exercise of protocol revision. Until then, we were changing our protocols in an ad hoc manner. We started doing it systematically by collecting feedback from all teammates and partner nephrologists, and collated this. We would send this to SAB members who would take the final call on what we would change and what would stay the same.

We then sent the new protocols to the nephrologists for their feedback, and after this thorough exercise, we released the new version for implementation.

This gave the protocols respectability and a seal of validity from experts. We called the protocols 'The NephroPlus Way'. We printed the protocols and had them put up on the walls at all the centres so that the staff could see them regularly and remember to follow them.

We also got into clinical research in a big way. We started analysing our data and publishing it in the form of abstracts, which were submitted to various national and international nephrology conferences. Our abstracts were selected at some of the most reputed conferences such as Indian Society of Nephrology, World Congress of Nephrology, European Renal Association, European Dialysis and Transplant Association and American Society of Nephrology. We presented our data at these conferences and received recognition as the only company from India that had this kind of data published at these conferences.

The advantage of our data was that the number of subjects was large, widely spread, as we had centres that spanned the length and breadth of the country, and it was data collected over an extended duration. This gave the data a lot of visibility and piqued the interest of several nephrologists and researchers.

We started doing clinical trials, academic studies and studies driven by clinicians and pharmaceutical companies.

Data collection was a very important initiative and came with its set of challenges. Staff at the centres had to do this additional work. We had to make it part of their regular work and not make it seem like more work. This was not done at other dialysis centres. At NephroPlus, they had to do it and did not get paid an additional amount for it. So, it was a tough task to get the staff to do it and do it accurately. We managed to a large extent. We kept improving the quality of our data year after year.

Another thing that Vikram strived for was to develop a healthy relationship with the press. As I have said before, none of us were publicity-crazy. We had no interest in getting our photos featured in newspapers or magazines. However, it is undeniable that this helps the business. We engaged with PR firms. They would make sure that the press would cover all major developments related to the company.

We were one of their easier clients. A healthcare company started by three young kids, one of whom had a personal connection to the cause, and was funded by marquee investment firms. What's not to like?

Most media houses were supportive and covered updates that we put out well. This resulted in NephroPlus becoming known by people we least expected to. We would get inbound inquiries from not only hospitals in the country but also governments and companies from outside India as well. They would want to explore partnerships, intrigued by the success they had read about.

Discipline was one of the most important aspects of the way we operated. We expected people to be exactly on time for calls and meetings. We expected emails to be responded to within twenty-four hours. People who couldn't adapt to this either left themselves or were politely asked to leave.

Vikram chiefly spearheaded these core aspects of the management of the company. He always ensured that everyone followed them and made sure this culture permeated to all levels. This was a very important contributor to the success of the company.

When people dealt with NephroPlus, we wanted them to see a professional, disciplined team that had above-board ethics and values.

All this groundwork laid the foundation for unbridled growth over the coming years. Whatever we did, wherever we went, we did not compromise on these core components of our culture.

* * *

One thing that was unique about NephroPlus was the way we engaged with nephrologists. We 'partnered' with nephrologists unlike some other companies in India, which 'employed' them. We were the only ones to offer them simulated equity as I outlined earlier. Over time, however, we found nephrologists less willing to invest in centres. We came up with various ways to make sure they contributed to the growth of the centres. The ethos of 'partnership' as opposed to 'employment' continued to be the cornerstone of our engagement with them. Soon, with a combination of various models, we had some of the country's top nephrologists on our partner list.

The medical community holds conferences for almost all disciplines where doctors from all over come together to attend a series of talks, presentations and discussions on various topics of common interest, including the latest developments in the field. Conferences can be domestic (where doctors from within the country attend) or international (where doctors from around the world attend). Over the years, however, these conferences have become notorious for doctors spending more time networking and sightseeing and less time attending academic sessions. Various pharmaceutical and device manufacturing companies set up stalls to showcase their drugs and products.

In the light of all this, in the middle of 2014, we wanted to have a conference where the clinical agenda would be of prime importance. There would be some networking and a bit of fun and sightseeing, but the primary purpose would be a series of strong clinical discussions. We debated various locations and then zeroed in on Bentota in Sri Lanka. It was a delightful resort town on the coast of Sri Lanka. We booked a few rooms at Vivanta by Taj for a two-night/two-day clinical retreat for all our nephrologist partners.

We planned a day-long solid clinical discussion and a few fun activities on the other day. We also decided to give out awards to the nephrologists whose centres had the best clinical outcomes.

Planning began. We invited all our partners. Most of them agreed to come. We engaged an event management company as this was the first time that we were doing such an event. Wanting to delight the nephrologists, we had a mix of talks on interesting topics, debates on contentious issues and one session on the future plans of the company. We had also planned an antakshari-like event on the first night.

Planning the entire event was quite a task. Doctors were flying into Colombo at various times from various locations. Some members of our team reached a couple of days before the event to ensure that all the arrangements were in place.

Sandeep and I were flying along with a group of doctors from Hyderabad. We were to take a flight to Chennai, from where we would board the flight to Colombo. We reached Chennai and headed towards the counter for the Colombo flight. They gave us the immigration slip to fill in our details. As I filled in the details, I opened up my passport and started writing the passport number and its expiry. That's when I noticed that the passport had already expired. I was wondering what was happening. I could feel droplets of sweat form on my scalp. My heart was racing. As I looked at the passport over and over again and checked all the pages, I realized what I had done. I had renewed my passport a few months ago. But when leaving for the conference, I had picked up my old passport instead of the new one. It was lying in my cupboard in Hyderabad.

Sandeep and I told the others who were travelling with us. We all started wondering what could be done. The flight to Colombo left in less than two hours. With a racing heart, I called my parents in Hyderabad and told them what had happened. We discussed various options like sending the new passport with the air hostess travelling on the next flight to Chennai and so on. Finally, the only thing that seemed workable was that Ram Murthy, someone who worked at my father's shop, would come with my passport by the next available flight and would hand it over to me at the Chennai airport. Unfortunately, this meant that I would reach Bentota only late at night as the next flight to Colombo was only in the evening. There simply was no other choice.

So, the rest of the team left. I was supposed to organize the antakshari event on the first day. All the files were on my laptop. I checked into a small hotel near the airport and waited for Ram Murthy to arrive at Chennai on his maiden flight. Using a combination of the hotel's patchy Wi-Fi and my cell phone's Internet connection, I uploaded the files to the cloud from where my colleague would download them so that they could conduct the antakshari.

I felt horrible as I was missing all the fun in Bentota.

My flight landed at Bentota late that night.

It was time for clinical discussions the next morning. I was the master of ceremonies. When the clock struck 9 a.m., Vikram took the microphone and welcomed the nephrologists. He was very particular that the programme begin on time and that all the nephrologists attend. He sent multiple messages to them that morning stating that timely attendance was mandatory. What followed were intense talks and debates on a variety of clinical topics. Some nephrologists complained that the programme was much too focused on clinical topics. They would have preferred something lighter. But Vikram would not have it any other way. While this may have ticked some people off, I think it helped cement the perception that we meant business and that our programmes would be unlike most other conferences.

We gave them a small gift to take back home at the end of the day-long deliberations.

That evening, we hosted an awards night recognizing those nephrologists whose centres had the best clinical outcomes. What was telling is that not one award was for the centre with the highest revenue or profits. The only awards were for clinical outcomes. This demonstrated that clinical outcomes were what we cared about the most.

On the last day, once all the events were over, Vikram, Sandeep and I walked over to the beach and chatted about the entire event, how well it had gone and how good the response was. After about an hour, close to midnight, we went back towards the hotel when it suddenly started raining. Vikram and Sandeep instinctively started running. I called out to them and said, 'We should just get wet tonight!' They laughed, came back and joined me. For the next half hour, the three of us stood in the rain and got completely drenched, laughing and joking the entire time.

We then went back to our rooms, dried up and met in my room for a steaming hot cup of tea. It was almost 2 a.m. when we retired.

The next day, as the nephrologists were leaving to go back home, each one of them commended us for the way the event had been organized. They could clearly see the difference between the regular conferences they kept attending and this one. Another thing that stood out was that this was like an 'exclusive club'. It was only for NephroPlus partners. No one else could attend.

We repeated this retreat in Goa a couple more times. Goa was simpler in terms of logistics, as there was a direct flight from almost every location in India. The format of the retreat remained largely the same, with one full day of clinical talks and debates; awards for outcomes and an evening of entertainment.

* * *

Twenty-eight-year-old Alok Shembekar* from Pune had won many medals in track and field events at the state level when he was in school and college. After completing his engineering, he took up a job in the city. Shortly after that, he discovered he had kidney disease because of uncontrolled hypertension. It was silent. He had no clue until it damaged his kidneys. It all happened so suddenly that in about three months, Alok's life changed from that of a diligent office-goer to a non-compliant dialysis patient.

After about a year on dialysis, he was so dejected with life that he no longer nurtured any hope of returning to running.

For Chennai-based Vasanthi Ganesan*, a forty-three-year-old mother of three and wife of a sales executive at a multinational FMCG company, badminton was the sport of choice. So, after a diagnosis of polycystic kidney disease in 2010, when she had to get on to dialysis, she missed her daily evening game of badminton with the other ladies from the colony, more than even a normal diet and fluid intake.

Most dialysis patients lack the energy to play sports actively. The mental and physical fatigue after a session is just too much for them to find the energy to lug their body for some physical exercise. There are some who take up a sport. This leads me to suspect that mental fatigue contributes more to this resistance than physical fatigue. While rapid fluid removal is a major cause for one to feel drained after a dialysis session, and there are factors like anaemia and bone disorders that prevent physically demanding activities among dialysis patients, we cannot deny the psychological dimension to this resistance.

We had done several Aashayein events by 2014—in Bengaluru, Agra, Delhi, and one more in Hyderabad. One day, Vikram came up with the idea of having an Olympics-style games event for dialysis patients. I am not sure how and when he got this idea. It may have come to him after he read about the Transplant Games, an Olympics-style event for kidney transplant recipients that are held in different parts of the world and India as well. He mentioned this to us and we were all excited about it. It would be a monumental event. No one in the world had organized anything like that ever.

The reasoning was that there was no reason why dialysis patients should not play a sport. There would be some patients with clinical problems that would not allow them to take part, but there would be several others who could. And we could always have less-intensive events like chess and carrom for patients with major mobility issues.

The plan was to have an Olympics-style event where dialysis patients from all over the country would come down to Hyderabad and take part in sporting events such as running, cycling, badminton, table tennis, basketball, etc. We decided to have it in Hyderabad after considering various locations such as Delhi, Mumbai and Pune. We felt organizing an event of this scale would be most convenient in Hyderabad as we were all there. There would be several things to figure out such as the venue, sponsors, travel and even dialysis for those who might need it.

We debated if we should do the event over one day or more. My initial thought was that we would need two days to organize the various events and have a proper set of finals. However, we decided against it since for patients coming from out of town, staying for two days would mean that most of them would need dialysis. We decided to do it on a Sunday. The event would be open to anyone on dialysis irrespective of whether they were getting their dialysis at a NephroPlus centre or not.

Many people from locations other than Hyderabad would be interested in such an event. But they would be hesitant because of the expense and the distance. We then took a bold decision. We decided to sponsor flight tickets for five patients from each major city. The first five to register from each of those cities would be extended this benefit.

The venue was finalized. The Kotla Vijaya Bhaskara Reddy Stadium in Hyderabad was available. It had a nice inner enclosure, which we could use for all the indoor games and a good track outside for outdoor events. It was centrally located.

We announced the date of the event after the venue was booked. It was to be held on 15 February 2015. We created a registration form and publicized it through our website and social media platforms. We informed the entire team about the event. They were all excited. People started registering.

We formed teams for various activities, such as travel, organizing the games, procuring the medals, engaging sponsors and so on.

One important aspect to be thought through was medical emergencies. Granted that patients were coming to take part in a sporting event, so they would be fit. However, we had to be prepared for any eventuality. We would need to track their vitals and also check their lungs using a stethoscope for any signs of fluid overload.

We decided to give each participant a T-shirt with a bib, which would have their registration number. It would just be easier to coordinate various activities with that arrangement.

We also decided to have pre-packed meals for breakfast and lunch, as our experience showed that managing a buffet meal involving a large crowd of people was always a challenge. We had our dietician plan the menus and talk to the caterer. They would provide separate salt packets, as all the food would be salt-free.

As the day approached, we roped in sponsors for the event as well. Registrations were also picking up. We had almost 500 registrations and there were still several days left for the event. Several people were from other cities. There was a huge buzz among dialysis circles all over the country.

Alok Shembekar got to know about the Olympiad from a technician in his dialysis centre in Pune. The technician knew about Alok's passion for running. He encouraged Alok to register. Alok dismissed the suggestion. It was all too much for him. Going to Hyderabad. How would he manage dialysis? What about the running? How would he run after so many years? Here he was struggling to get through each day with all the complications around the treatment. Running at a fancy event in Hyderabad was not in the realm of possibility.

Vasanthi Ganesan saw our post on Facebook. Her heart fluttered when she saw badminton among the listed sport activities. Could she do it? She thought about it over the next couple of days without mentioning it to her family. How could she manage? She hadn't gone out of Chennai for several years. Would she need to practise? She couldn't just land up at the stadium and play. Who would help her practise?

Alok eventually realized that this was the best opportunity for him to get back to running. He spoke to his nephrologist, who supported him. Alok signed up for the event and started practising. He began with a gentle jog. Every passing day would see him adding speed and distance. He felt energetic for the first time in years. He started imagining himself getting on to the podium and donning the gold medal.

Vasanthi finally spoke to her husband and he sounded even more excited than her. The entire family would go to Hyderabad and cheer her. She called her friends and told them about the event. They started jumping with excitement. Vasanthi had to calm them down and ask them to practise with her. Every evening, they would play with Vasanthi. At first, it was difficult. Years of little or no physically strenuous activities cause the muscles to waste away. It takes tremendous effort and determination to get them to work again. That was something Vasanthi did not lack. She signed up using the online form we had posted on Facebook.

In the meantime, in Hyderabad, we set up a 'War Room'. Leave it to a consultant to give it a fancy name! We formed a team to review the various aspects of organizing the event. The team would meet every day at a particular time and take stock. Regular folks would just have a 'meeting'. But a consultant has to call it a war room. Well, whatever works.

In the last week before the event, the excitement peaked. We had a countdown on social media. People posted pictures from railway stations and airports as they embarked on the trip to Hyderabad. It looked as though we were on to something here. We conducted several mock drills on how to transport patients on a stretcher in case they had a complication. We also arranged for two ambulances to be stationed at the stadium should a patient need to be transferred to a hospital in case of serious complications.

One thing we realized a few days before the event was that there was an India-Pakistan World Cup match on the same day. We were all worried. Would this affect attendance? We decided to have two large screens that would show the match live so that people would not miss the event for the match.

Patients started arriving a couple of days prior. They had already arranged for dialysis at our centres. I met some of them and could feel their excitement about participating in the event.

The Olympiad couldn't have been a more apt event for us. Our vision was to enable people to lead a normal life. What makes up a normal life, really? To me, it means to do things healthy people do. Like work, travel, exercise, go out for a movie and hang out with friends. Another important part of a normal life is physical exercise. Many dialysis patients give up on all kinds of physical exertion after getting on to dialysis. A small number do simple exercises like walking or yoga. An ever smaller number play a sport.

It needn't be that way. There are several patients who stretch themselves to the limit. Take the case of Shad Ireland from the US. A dialysis patient, he has done the Iron Man twice!

Wikipedia describes the Iron Man[2] as:

'An Ironman Triathlon is one of a series of long-distance triathlon races organized by the World Triathlon Corporation (WTC), consisting of a 2.4-mile (3.86 km) swim, a 112-mile (180.25 km) bicycle ride and a marathon 26.22-mile (42.20 km) run, raced in that order.'

This would be very difficult even for people with healthy kidneys. But Shad Ireland, a dialysis patient, has done it twice over.

He's not alone. There is also Maddy Warren from the UK who ran the London Marathon in 2018.

The point is that dialysis doesn't prevent you from exercising or taking up a sport. It is the thought that you are on dialysis that prevents you. It is not the body, but the mind.

This negativity was what we were attempting to challenge among Indian dialysis patients. The Olympiad was an invitation to all those patients who were doing some form of physical exercise or had taken up a sport to come and inspire the rest. This was also an invitation to all those who had given up on a sport after getting hooked to the dialysis machine. It was an opportunity to awaken those sleeping dragons within. This was the chance of a lifetime to grab their life back and show the world and more importantly, themselves, that they could lead a normal life.

The first Indian Dialysis Olympiad was upon us. The night before, we all went to the stadium to see it being readied for the event. Various branding elements of our company and the sponsors were being put up. We inspected the locations of the various sporting events. It looked like we were all set.

I went back home. My body ached from all the exertion of the day. My mind was racing, thinking about the event the next day. I did not have dialysis that night. I tried to keep my mind at rest, trying not to think of anything. My body was also yearning for the rest that only sleep can offer.

* * *

I woke up the next morning, fresh and energetic. I got ready and went to the venue. Everyone from the team was already there. The stadium was buzzing with activity.

People started arriving from 8 a.m. onwards. Patients were very excited. They registered, got bibs with their participant number, a welcome kit that had some coupons for food and gifts, and made their way to the seating area.

I met Alok Shembekar and Vasanthi Ganesan at the breakfast counter. They were barely able to contain their excitement. In unison, they thanked NephroPlus for coming up with this idea and putting in so much effort to organize it. I thanked them for taking the trouble to come for the event from far away.

The games began at around 9 a.m. and within an hour, all the sporting events had started. While the sensible thing would have been to stay put on the chair in the corner, I could hardly contain myself. I made my way, one by one, to the various games areas and watched as patients battled it out for the medals.

People of all ages were taking part in the activities. Many of them had not played a game after getting on dialysis. They were all here to prove a point.

Before they could participate in a contest, the patients had to get their vitals checked at the counter designated for the purpose. Our clinical staff assessed their blood pressure and pulse, and examined their chest with a stethoscope to check if there was any obvious fluid overload. We found some patients who had high blood pressure. When they were told that they could not contest, they protested. They said they had come all the way to Hyderabad for the event and that we could not disallow them. We explained to them that this was in their own interest. We suggested that they relax for a while and then come back to get their pressure checked. While some people managed to reduce their pressure with some rest, there were some who had to be refused on safety grounds.

While those who were younger or fitter played games involving physical activity, we had also arranged for activities like carrom, sudoku and chess for those who wanted to take part in this historic event but could not undertake too much physical exertion. It was heartening to see an elderly patient play carrom as part of the Olympiad. It was her way of saying she would not miss out on all the fun!

We paused the games around lunch. Doing packed meals was an excellent idea as lunch went on without any commotion. Once we wound up lunch, the games resumed. By around 3 p.m., we completed the final rounds of all the games.

After the games, we organized a small Aashayein-like event where some doctors spoke. We had some antakshari games as well which people took part in with vigour despite the exhaustion that the games might have brought upon them. After this was the medal ceremony where we presented the top three players in each sport with gold, silver and bronze medals in true Olympic style. We had some nephrologist partners—who had been flown in from different locations and from within Hyderabad as well—give away the medals.

Both Alok and Vasanthi won medals that day. They met me after the event, before heading back home and promised to keep in touch. I could see their eyes gleaming with pride.

The theme of the event, highlighted in all our marketing collaterals, was 'Kidney failure did not take away their Will to Win'. That sentence aptly summarized the event. Each participant also wore a T-shirt that said, 'I have the Will to Win'.

When kidney disease strikes, it takes a huge toll on the individual. It affects every organ of the body, but the organ that is impacted the most is the brain. While there is also a physiological impact on the body, the psychological impact is even more evident. People become depressed and lose interest in life. They believe that life as they know it has ended. They find their dreams being shattered.

Events such as these help in enabling people to find themselves. Such initiatives bring a whiff of fresh air into their lives. They have something to look forward to. They begin to want success in something as small as badminton or cycling. This sets them up for larger battles in life. Having played something that is the prerogative only of 'healthy' people, they find, within themselves, renewed confidence. They suddenly believe they are capable of more.

The peer effect also works beautifully here. All around them they see people with a similar affliction as theirs. All engaged in battles. Not only with their opponent in a sporting match but against life itself. Even if they lose the match against their opponent, they are winning the more important battle—that for their life. This eggs them on. They push themselves harder.

Long after the Olympiad, when they went back to their daily lives, they were inspired to do more. Many of them took up a sport. Some got back to work. All of them, however, cherished the memories of that one day in February when winter was easing away and summer was just shy of blazing in, when they decided that they also had the 'Will to Win'.

* * *

When a company grows rapidly, as we were doing then, some things go wrong. The focus shifted to growth. Everyone in the company was geared towards it.

At one point, we started feeling a rumbling within the organization. It is difficult to put into words what exactly it was. But we knew something was amiss. It felt as if we were running a production line. New centres were getting added. Staff was getting hired. Guests would keep increasing. Operationally, things were fine. The numbers did not indicate a problem.

When we visited a centre, though, we could see some early signs of trouble. Staff were going about their work mechanically. Centres, especially the initial ones, were not looking so nice any more. Files were strewn all over. The paint from the walls was peeling. What was worse was that people didn't seem to care.

The rate at which we had added centres was making it difficult for the rest of the team to keep pace. While the business development team signed up new hospitals and nephrologists, the other teams had to work that much harder to do the other bits that enabled us to launch these centres.

The team that did the build-out work—some civil, plumbing and electrical work, branding and so on—had to contend with managing this work for several centres at the same time. The HR team had to hire more and more people to manage the centres. Transition of operations at multiple centres, both administrative and clinical, had to be done by the operations and clinical teams. All the teams were getting stretched.

It was slowly becoming evident.

We, the management team, had a meeting. We felt we had to do something. Arrest the apathy before it became unmanageable. Even if it came at the cost of growth. Several ideas were discussed. Everyone in the room realized that our success was becoming dangerous!

We had to pause and review. We had to stop adding new centres and fix the problems before continuing to grow. Once the maddening rush to get the new centres on board would ebb, the team could consolidate, brainstorm and put in place processes and perhaps, new teams, to ensure that we were able to comfortably add new centres while ensuring existing centres got the love they needed.

While this was a scary proposition—our competitors could get ahead of us—we felt that if we didn't do it then, it might be too late. We did not want to build a company that relied only on numbers. We had to make sure the soul was not lost.

So, we took the courageous decision of stopping all new centre transitions. We set up teams that would look into every aspect of all the problems we were facing and come up with ways in which we could address them.

We set up a new transition team. This would comprise two new roles—transition centre managers and transition technicians. The sole responsibility of these people would be to bring new centres into the purview of NephroPlus. They would spend one to three months in new centres and train newly hired individuals or staff retained from the old team that was running the centre till we came in, in all aspects of the 'NephroPlus Way' of doing things. We moved our capable centre managers and technicians who were willing to travel continuously (for an incentive) to this team.

To ensure we had independent teams to manage up to four new centre build-outs at the same time, we also bolstered our build-out team.

In addition, we instituted a 'Kick-off call' for every new centre signed. Representatives from all functions would attend this call where the BD team would summarize the terms of the deal of the new centre and the plan for the transition would be drawn up.

We also undertook an exercise where older centres were beautified. This could include simple things like a coat of paint and change of banners outside or a more thorough revamp of the centre where some carpentry or plumbing work was taken up.

This entire exercise took us about three months during which no new centres were signed up. The BD team kept those leads warm to ensure they did not go to anyone else.

At the end of this exercise, when we felt we had things under control, we resumed adding centres while closely monitoring our centres to see how we were doing.

After another three months, we could say the pause had worked. We were ambling along with no signs of distress. The issues that we had seen in the past seemed to have settled.

This was a counter-intuitive decision. We were worried about how it might impact growth. In our minds, though, there was no other way out. We did not want to simply add centres without ensuring that the core remained intact. Our guests could not get a different experience than the one we intended. Adding numbers meant little if we did not continue to delight our guests.

Even business-wise, this decision made sense. We were clear about our value-add in the dialysis ecosystem. If we lost that, why would dialysis patients opt for NephroPlus? Why would our guests continue with us? Nephrologists would also stop sending their patients to our centres. The numbers wouldn't hold without this.

We realized it was important to never let go of the basics: the reason we were where we were. Temporary setbacks were all right. We mustn't, however, lose sight of the long-term goal and vision of the company. The reason why we exist.

* * *

11

Our Boat Is Rocked

'If we had no winter, the spring would not be so pleasant.
If we did not sometimes taste of adversity, prosperity would not be so welcome.'
—Anne Bradstreet

By early 2015, we had about sixty centres. Realizing that we needed more money to fund our plans for the growth path that we were on, we started searching for investors yet again. There was a lot of interest from several marquee PE companies. We started preparing the pitch deck and sending it out to different companies. Vikram started meeting some of them after an initial conversation. A few also came down to our office to meet with the team.

Around the same time, we got to know that one of India's largest and most reputed hospital chains was in discussions with DaVita to run their dialysis centres. I will call them Healthium*. Founded in 2001 by two brothers, it soon became one of India's premium hospital brands and spread beyond, to countries in the Asia-Pacific region as well.

DaVita was the US's second-largest dialysis provider network. Fresenius was the largest. Together, these two companies owned a large part of the US dialysis market. Fresenius had the unique advantage of being one of the world's largest dialysis machine and consumables manufacturers and this vertical integration gave them an advantage that others simply did not have.

DaVita had entered India by acquiring a company called NephroLife, headquartered in Bengaluru and started by two entrepreneurs, Shriram Vijaykumar and Dev Roy. They had two or three centres when they got acquired by DaVita. Shriram continued to manage operations for a while before moving on to take a larger role in the Asia-Pacific geography of the company. They hired local talent to run the company. They grew at an easy pace and had about twenty centres. This was in sharp contrast to our sixty centres, when both companies had started around the same time.

DaVita was already running the dialysis centre at Healthium's flagship hospital in Gurgaon, which is part of the National Capital Region that encompasses Delhi. They wanted to extend that partnership to all Healthium hospitals. We wanted to pitch to Healthium for this as well. Very few hospitals could match the reputation of the Healthium group as a hospital chain. We found some contacts in Healthium and made the pitch to them.

For the next several months, these two major projects would run side-by-side—the Series C fundraise and the Healthium deal. They were both massive initiatives and required a lot of effort from the management team.

For the investment round, after several gruelling meetings involving various members of our team, visits to centres and a lot of rounds of deliberations, we had zeroed in on four investors who seemed like frontrunners. For the sake of protecting their confidentiality, I will call them InvestNow*, Highway*, Comprehend* and TuskForce*.

InvestNow is a very old and large investment firm. Owned by a billionaire family, the company is headquartered in the US and has a few trillion dollars in assets under management.

The other three companies had more modest backgrounds.

Highway was a healthcare-focused fund operating in the Asia-Pacific region and had a few billion dollars in assets under management.

Comprehend was a much more recently-founded fund, headed by a few reputed people formerly from one of the world's leading PE firms. They had no investments as yet but had the tag of their previous company and that was enough for many people.

TuskForce, which was based out of Mumbai, connected with us through one of Vikram's contacts who worked there.

A bookie would give InvestNow the highest odds of bagging the deal. However, we were not dreamy-eyed about them investing in us. We would consider several factors before deciding.

We requested all of them to submit non-binding offers. Based on these offers, we would go into the next phase of diligence with the company that made the best offer.

In the meantime, the Healthium team decided that they would explore outsourcing their dialysis centres to us as well. They continued discussions with DaVita while beginning conversations with us. Their team visited some of our centres. I flew down to Delhi and met with their head of clinical affairs and their main clinical team, along with some of our doctors. We had spoken to Dr Vivek Jha, our chief medical officer, Dr Satish Chhabra and Dr Deepak Dewan, both consulting nephrologists at our centres, and requested them to join us for the meeting.

The meeting with the Healthium clinical team went very well. We showcased our processes and innovations. I was almost standing for the entire duration of the meeting, handing out documents describing how we did things differently. They felt the passion we had for our work.

That was one major difference between a company like DaVita and ours. While the employees of DaVita would treat this like any other job, for us, it was our life. We lived and breathed NephroPlus day in and day out. This difference would be quite clear in interactions with both parties.

In the meantime, the Series C term sheets came in. After examining all of them, we decided to go with InvestNow. They offered a better valuation. We signed the term sheet. The due diligence began.

After a lot of negotiations, we also finalized the terms of the Healthium deal. However, right before we signed it, the founder brothers came up with a strange request. They wanted equity in our company as part of the deal. This came as an enormous surprise to us.

On the one hand, it was the best validation we could ever receive in terms of the value of our company and what we were doing. That someone like the brothers would want a stake in our company rather than cash showed that they believed in our plans and expected us to have stellar growth.

On the other hand, would we be comfortable giving up equity to them?

The board met and brainstormed. The mandate was clear. We had to do this.

Vikram and Sandeep flew to Delhi and met one of the brothers over dinner and shook hands. They arrived at a mutually agreeable valuation. We would give them part of it upfront and the remaining as annuity (payments every year). We would also give them a small single-digit stake in the company. We signed the term sheet soon after.

We had two term sheets in hand. One was of a reputed PE company that had decided to invest in us at a very good valuation. The other was of India's most reputed hospital chain, which was going to outsource their dialysis centres to us.

Over the next several weeks, we began the diligence gathering exercise of the Healthium dialysis asset. What we discovered was quite alarming. The centres were all operating like independent units. Healthium had acquired most of their hospitals—not started them—and grown them organically. Though there was financial integration, there was almost no operational and clinical integration.

The thing that shocked us the most, however, was that the sample numbers that they gave us when we agreed on the valuation differed greatly from what was there on the ground. During the diligence exercise, we discovered that the sample numbers they gave us were chosen from two of their best-performing centres and hence, they were inflated when applied across the network.

We were not used to this. For us, numbers had always been sacred. We just do not over-project numbers. So, this came as an immense surprise. We reviewed the differences and came up with the revised valuation. We went back to Healthium and told them of our findings and the changed valuation, along with a proposal on how we would like to adjust the structure of the deal.

To our utter surprise, they stood their ground and said they would not brook any change in the deal structure, due diligence findings be damned.

We explained to them that what they were saying made little sense. How could the structure of the deal and the numbers be the same if the numbers they had promised differed materially from what they had committed in the initial exercise?

For us, not doing the deal would mean a reduction in the Series C valuation. However, after much deliberation, Vikram sent an email to the Healthium team stating that we were respectfully withdrawing from the deal. This probably came as a shock to the Healthium team, who had thought that we were desperate to do the deal. They had an inkling that we were in the middle of our fundraise and if we did not do the deal, the valuation of the company would go down. So, they were very confident that we would not just walk away.

For us, it was about doing the right thing. Yes, Healthium was big. Their centres would give a tremendous boost to the company. But we would start the relationship on a sour note. How would this impact the equation between the two parties in the long term?

As expected, walking away from the Healthium deal had a ripple effect on the Series C transaction as well. InvestNow revised the valuation downwards. The difference was huge. Though we had expected a downward revision, we did not think it would be that much. It seemed like they were taking advantage of the situation. They knew that we had stopped talking to the other investors. They felt that we would have no choice but to do the deal on whatever terms they offered.

Highway had not put in a proposal in the first round because of a time constraint. They could not get the necessary approvals from their LPs (limited partners, i.e., the individuals/ companies that invest funds in a PE with which the company makes investments). We reached out to them and said there was a window of opportunity where we were accepting another offer. They seemed excited and got back with an offer that was better than InvestNow's original offer as well. The game was on!

We told InvestNow that we were respectfully annulling the term sheet. They were shell-shocked. We were a tiny company. The investment climate was also quite negative. They reached out to us and other investors on our board to make amends to their proposal, but we did not budge.

We signed up with Highway, which was actually Sea Link Capital. Our funds were in place for the next round of expansion.

The significance of two such events within a brief span of time was not lost on anyone. We had spurned two big guys at once. An outside observer might have thought that we had grown too big too soon. What did we think? Who the hell were we?

The truth, however, is that both decisions were logical. It was the other party behaving like a bully. Trying to take advantage of our position. We were fortunate that our board was all right with both our decisions. What we did wasn't to heckle a bully. It was to do what our conscience felt was the right thing and not cow down to unreasonable power. We were relieved, though, that in the end, it had all worked out.

* * *

In Tenali district of Andhra Pradesh, thirty-two-year-old Savithri Amuktha* was waiting to see the doctor in the primary health centre (PHC) of the region. Her husband, Pratap*, was accompanying her. This was in May 2015. She had been feeling breathless and had noticed her feet had swollen for the past few weeks. The doctor said she would need to get a few tests done. They took the prescription, went to the district government hospital and gave the samples for testing.

After a couple of days, they went back to collect the results. They did not know what to make of them. They met the duty doctor there who told them, betraying no sign of emotion, that she had kidney disease. He also muttered something about dialysis.

They realized the magnitude of the problem when they went to the PHC and showed the reports to the doctor. The doctor asked them to sit while examining the reports. In Telugu, he explained to them that Savithri's kidneys had failed and that if she did not get dialysis, she would not survive for too long.

Savithri and her husband couldn't say a word. On the way home, both of them remained silent. How had this happened so suddenly? Did someone perform black magic? What did it mean? What was dialysis? How long will I need to do it? When will I become fine?

All these questions were arising in her mind. The doctor had said she would have to go to Guntur, where the closest hospital with dialysis facilities was located.

Then began Savithri's tryst with dialysis. Twice a week, she would pack a small bag and take a bus to Guntur, where she would get dialysis in the government hospital and come back. Her husband would accompany her sometimes, but, after a while, she insisted on going alone as her husband could not take so much time off from his job.

Hundreds of patients like Savithri, who live in non-metro cities and towns of India have a similar life. With no dialysis facility close to their homes, they would travel for hours every week just to get dialysis.

On the leap day of 2016, Finance Minister Arun Jaitley of the Narendra Modi government—that had been in power for less than two years then—made an unprecedented announcement in Parliament that would change the dialysis landscape in India like never before. He announced:

'To address (the abysmal dialysis access) situation, I propose to start a "National Dialysis Services Programme". Funds will be made available through PPP mode under the National Health Mission, to provide dialysis services in all district hospitals. To reduce the cost, I propose to exempt certain parts of dialysis equipment from basic customs duty, excise/CVD and SAD.'

This meant that the poorest of the poor in India could finally get dialysis treatment, something they had been denied for decades just because they could not afford it. The union government said that they would fund dialysis sessions in all district hospitals. The states would implement it through the PPP route and the union government would reimburse them. They had thought through this fairly well. They came up with draft guidelines of floating tenders along with quality criteria and payment norms.

This was probably the first time that the phrase 'dialysis services' appeared in the Union Budget. It had been that badly neglected by successive governments. There were rumours, which were later confirmed, that Arun Jaitley himself suffered from kidney disease. He was a chronic diabetic. Perhaps the plight of dialysis patients came to his notice, and he had decided to do something about it.

Over the next few years, he and another very important minister in the Narendra Modi government, Sushma Swaraj, would be diagnosed with end-stage kidney failure, have kidney transplants and die a few years after their surgeries. Arun Jaitley died a year later and Sushma Swaraj three years after her surgery. Never before had the country's collective attention been drawn so starkly towards kidney disease and its aftermath. Sceptics raised questions on how the two ministers got unrelated donor kidneys when the waiting list for common citizens was so long. However, among government circles, these two high-profile patients ensured people paid a lot of attention to kidney failure and dialysis.

The government of Andhra Pradesh was the first to adopt the National Dialysis Services programme.

At NephroPlus, we were very excited by these developments. Our pet peeve was affordability in India. Only a small proportion of patients who needed dialysis were getting it. This could change the scene. Yes, the money per session would be minuscule. But the volumes would be huge.

One major factor to be considered was that we would deal with the government much more than ever before. Our exposure to governments was limited until then. This would change that. The volume would be huge and there would be potential for expansion.

We had to make a well-thought-through decision. More state governments would launch similar projects in the future. Would we apply for them as well? Why or why not?

One major factor we considered was the governance and corruption of various state governments. We had no tolerance for corrupt government officials. We would want billing dues to be cleared centrally and transparently.

During the pre-bid meeting where interested bidders come together to seek and request clarifications or additions to bid terms, several providers attended. Vikram represented NephroPlus. He made the startling suggestion that the government should add a clause that penalized the provider for every seroconversion—patient being infected with an infectious virus like hepatitis C or B—that occurred because of the provider's fault. This shocked the rest of the providers who were present. A provider was requesting the addition of a suggestion that was not in their favour.

Had Vikram gone mad? What was NephroPlus thinking?

Our logic was simple. Cross-infections are a curse at dialysis centres. We had to do everything in our power to prevent them. If we won the tender, we were confident of our abilities to prevent cross-infections as we took this seriously. Even if we did not win, the same criteria would apply to the other providers and, in the end, patients would benefit. We suggested that there be adequate safeguards to ensure that they penalized the provider only if cross-infection was their fault. If it happened because of reasons beyond their control, then there should be no penalty.

This was a pattern that repeated in pre-bid meetings for almost all PPP projects both within and outside India over the coming years. While other providers would request terms that made the tender more lenient, NephroPlus would suggest several measures to improve the tender so that it benefited patients, even if the terms made it more difficult and expensive for the provider.

The government of Andhra Pradesh incorporated the suggestions we made, to the letter.

We started working on the bid. Vikram, Sandeep and the various teams got down to analysing what the lowest possible bid should be to ensure we bagged the tender. The key was volumes. The centres would run to capacity. Of that, we were confident. We were worried about the working capital cost as governments in India usually delay payments.

One differentiating factor in this project, and indeed, all projects to be rolled out under the Free Dialysis Programme, as it would be called, was that for all patients who were carriers of the hepatitis C, hepatitis B or the HIV viruses and needed dialysis, the dialysers would not be reprocessed.

Dialyser reprocessing was a cost-saving measure used in several countries, including the US, where a dialyser—the artificial kidney used to filter the blood of water and toxins—was cleaned thoroughly and sterilized after one treatment and reused again for the next treatment of the same patient. This was done until the efficiency of the dialyser fell below a certain threshold. The efficiency was measured by a parameter called the fibre bundle volume (FBV), which was the amount of blood that could be held by the dialyser. In our network, we had decided that the threshold to reuse a dialyser was that the FBV should not be less than 80 per cent of the original. Effectively, this ensured that over 80 per cent efficiency was always maintained.

The tender issued by the government of Andhra Pradesh had an FBV cut-off of 70 per cent. This, however, would be only for those patients who were not carriers of the three viruses. For those who were carriers, the dialyser could be used only once and then discarded.

Not reusing dialysers for virus carriers was an excellent method of avoiding cross-infections with these viruses.

The tender bid price would have to account for the different reuse models for carriers and non-carriers. The price paid by the government would be the same irrespective of whether or not the patient was a carrier. So, the provider had to estimate what proportion of patients would be carriers as the cost of these treatments would be significantly higher than treatments for non-carriers.

After determining various factors that affected the cost, the teams came up with a very competitive price for the tender. This was a very low number. It was possible only because the volumes would be high.

We submitted the bid. Now all we could do was wait.

After several weeks of waiting, the announcement came. We had won! We were ecstatic. Our competitors had bid higher than us. Perhaps we had the benefit of size compared to them. This was going to be a new beginning in the company's life.

PPP projects would become a major part of the company's focus. Our way of thinking would have to change since we would need to focus on receivables. Any delay in receiving money would cause trouble. The money for dialysis, until then, was all received before treatment. For PPP projects, we would receive money several weeks after the treatment. Working capital could suddenly become a challenge. The mindset of the company would require quite a transformation. We rose to the challenge. Vikram, realizing this early on, instructed Vaibhav Joshi, the finance controller, to set up a separate accounts receivable (AR) team whose sole job would be to ensure that the AR from various projects did not go beyond a particular number.

Vikram was brilliant in this respect. He saw these things coming, came up with a solution and implemented it just like a cheetah spots, follows and pounces on its prey.

On 26 August 2016, the health minister of the state of Andhra Pradesh inaugurated the new dialysis centre in Tenali's government hospital. Vikram attended the event. The scenes were reminiscent of the launch of our Mahabubnagar centre. A lot of patients had heard about the new centre and had come to see it.

Savithri and Pratap had come too. They were very excited about the quality of the centre. It looked as swanky as a private hospital, and was a ten-minute walk from their home, compared to the hour-long bus journey they had to undertake till then. Life would no longer be the same.

Savithri was one of the first patients to register at the centre and begin dialysis. I spoke to her over Skype one afternoon during her dialysis session. She was thrilled to be getting dialysis so close to home and the infrastructure at the centre and dialysis quality were beyond her wildest imagination.

I felt nice speaking to her that day. I was convinced that we were doing the right thing. It was challenging to run this kind of distributed network. Every day brought fresh problems for us to solve. Anything can happen in a centre. This is a medical process with a lot of risks. There was constant stress.

However, when you have one call with a guest who compliments the excellent work that you are doing, that can act like a balm for the aching soul. It can make you feel that all the stress is worth it. You get renewed energy to work harder and improve the output even further. When you hear how you have changed their life, given them a better quality of life and made them more productive, just by providing good-quality dialysis, you feel grateful that you are able to do this and you can ask for no better job in the world.

* * *

People start a company for various reasons. Some want to solve an existing problem that has not been solved before, while some want to solve the problem in better ways than others have done in the past. Some people do it because they want to get rich after hearing stories about successful start-ups.

Vikram started NephroPlus because he found many areas in Indian healthcare that could be done better. Dialysis was one of them. I joined hands with Vikram because I believe dialysis can be done better. Sandeep joined us because he is a serial entrepreneur. He enjoyed being in start-ups. He liked the raw energy that start-ups demanded and produced.

Most start-up founders make tremendous sacrifices in their journey. Their families as well. Manju, Vikram's wife, gave up her career so that she could bring in some stability and be there for Vikram when he needed her. Sandeep got married to Divya Kalva, an IT professional, a few years after the birth of NephroPlus. Divya had to make sacrifices in her career as well to make sure Sandeep got to pursue his dream in NephroPlus.

There may have been several incidents in Vikram and Sandeep's lives that I am not even aware of, enabling them to continue living their dream in this company at the expense of their family lives. I did not have to make any such sacrifices since I am unmarried and I could not take any chances with my medical treatment.

As part of her job, Divya got opportunities to go to the US on work. Her company even asked her to move there. Moving to the US is a dream for many IT professionals. Divya refused because she realized that it would put a strain on their family and that was not ideal.

At one point, Sandeep started feeling guilty that Divya had to sacrifice her career for his role in the company. By that time, they also had two kids. NephroPlus had stabilized as a company by then. Having completed two rounds of funding and running over fifty centres, we were all set for the next phase of growth. He probably missed the uncertainty of a start-up environment, however crazy that might sound.

After a lot of thought, he broached the topic with us one evening and said Divya had been asked, yet again, to move to the US. While she was ready to forego the opportunity again, he felt it would not be right because she had sacrificed her career for his multiple times. This time, he felt he should move on. He would be ready to support us in whatever manner possible. Remotely, he would continue to advise us on various things.

Vikram and I were quite disturbed for a few days. The three of us had started this company together. Any of us leaving was a setback. We couldn't imagine NephroPlus without even one of us.

At the same time, Vikram fully empathized with Sandeep's situation. He always felt guilty about being indirectly responsible for Manju giving up her career. We had several conversations in the days that followed about any other potential solutions. We could not think of anything and came to terms with his decision.

A few months after that, Sandeep quit NephroPlus in an executive capacity and switched to an advisory role. He and Divya flew to the US. Divya began working and Sandeep started looking for a job. Things didn't quite work out there with changing visa rules under Donald Trump and they had to return to India.

We had already hired Rohit Singh, in the meantime, to take Sandeep's place as head of business development. It took Rohit a few months to settle down, during which the number of new deals signed had reduced. But soon, we regained our momentum.

Under normal circumstances, Sandeep would have found a job and settled down in the US. However, the Donald Trump presidency changed all that. The US government changed rules related to spouses of people on a work visa. The new rules meant Sandeep could not work. They explored various ways but nothing was working out. In less than a year, Sandeep and his family returned to India.

Sandeep's close friend, Raghuraj Sunder Raju, from Bengaluru, had started a mobile app and data analytics company, Healthplix. Raghuraj pitched to Sandeep to join his company as the CEO. Raghuraj knew that Sandeep, with his extensive experience in NephroPlus and from before, would steer the company to great heights. After a lot of deliberation, Sandeep agreed to join Healthplix.

I sorely missed Sandeep's presence in the company. We had a very good equation. Sandeep had an amazing ability to think out of the box. When most of us would come up with routine ideas, Sandeep had the ability to think up something completely novel. Something very brave and radical.

Despite no such proclamations in public or private, I am fairly certain that Vikram also missed Sandeep in NephroPlus. He had always relied on Sandeep and his business sense for sounding out various ideas. They both discussed and decided on almost everything.

I was very naïve with the business side of things and added little value on decisions related to BD strategies and financial aspects like valuation of the company during fundraises or how to get good debt from banks and other financial institutions. I took responsibility for the clinical aspects and IT. So, after Sandeep left, Vikram probably missed his inputs. When you have to take such major decisions, it is very useful to have someone to talk it over with. Even if it may be just to validate your ideas.

* * *

12

The Winner Takes It All

'The winner takes it all
The loser's standing small
Beside the victory
That's her destiny'
—Benny Andersson/Björn K. Ulvaeus, ABBA

HealthTec* is a large medical device manufacturer. Headquartered in the US, they started working on a portable haemodialysis machine in early 2010. Their intent was to launch the machine in the Indian Subcontinent once it was ready. Some people attributed their interest in the subcontinent to lenient regulations, which made it convenient to first try the machine in less stringent conditions and subsequently take it to developed countries. I did not believe the rumours though and felt the company genuinely wanted to launch in south Asia because of the sore need for quality dialysis.

We got an inquiry from one of their senior executives, Raj Varma*, on 5 October 2012. He had left a comment on our website's Contact Us page. He mentioned that they were working on an affordable, portable haemodialysis machine and wanted to speak to our nephrologists about the product concept. All inquiries on the Contact Us page came to me. I responded to him stating that I was a patient myself and that the concept they were working on was exciting. I offered to set up a meeting with our nephrologists and our team in Hyderabad.

Raj was of Indian origin and had graduated in science from India before moving to the US and completing his PhD there. He joined HealthTec soon after and had been there ever since. Shortly, he began heading the kidney care division of the company.

We met Raj on 2 March 2013 at 7 p.m. at the Waterside Cafe in Hyderabad's Taj Banjara. Dr Krishnan, our nephrologist partner from our second centre in Secunderabad, Dr Kavitha Gone, who was covering our Banjara Hills centre at the time, Vikram and I met him for dinner. The conversation lingered around dialysis in India, the sore need for innovation in the dialysis space and the growth of NephroPlus.

Raj shared some details of their dialysis machine. He said that the machine would solve one of the biggest problems in India—scarcity of water and the enormous bandwidth and cost that providers have to bear for setting up water treatment plants. He claimed their machine could do a full four-hour dialysis session with one litre of bottled water. Several people around the table gasped when they heard that statement.

That would be an enormous accomplishment if it were true. A haemodialysis session requires about 400 litres of raw water. The water treatment plants that we had in our network were typically operating at a rejection rate of 50 per cent, which meant that you needed about twice the amount of raw water as the amount of treated water needed for a dialysis session.

In the months preceding that March dinner with Raj, we had seen some serious issues with our water treatment plants, especially in rural areas like Mahabubnagar. We were spending enormous amounts of money to keep the plant running to give us the desired quality of water as output.

This came as welcome news to me. It would make operations significantly less challenging. We wouldn't even need a water treatment plant. We could just get bottles of mineral water widely available in India and carry out the sessions.

When Raj asked Vikram about water treatment plants and the challenges they posed, Vikram made light of the entire issue. He said that water treatment plants were hardly a challenge. Raj was quite startled as this differed from what he had heard until then. He had spoken to several Indian nephrologists in the past and all of them were quite clear that water was a major challenge in the dialysis ecosystem. Vikram probably said this to not give them an edge in any future negotiations.

The meeting ended on a positive note, though, with a promise to keep in touch and discuss ways and means of collaborating in the future.

We kept in touch sporadically over the next few years. They kept us updated on how the development of their machine was coming along. The progress was agonizingly slow, as was expected in a product of this nature. They sounded us off from time to time and sought inputs on various aspects of the machine as well.

On 2 September 2016, about three and a half years after that dinner, all of a sudden, I received an email from Raj. He mentioned that he had been following our growth and was quite impressed. He also said that they had made significant progress on various fronts and proposed an initial call and in-person meeting soon to discuss ways in which we could collaborate.

I assumed it had to do with their HD machine. I got back to him, and a few email exchanges later, we had frozen on a date and time for the call. Raj called me on the evening of 7 September. The call turned out differently from what I had expected.

While he apprised me about the machine and the progress that they had made over the years, the real reason came up a few minutes into the call. Candidly, Raj mentioned they were looking at acquiring NephroPlus!

I was shocked. I wasn't ready for this at all. He put me at ease and said that he understood that this might have come as a surprise to me, but HealthTec wanted to get into services and they thought NephroPlus was best placed for them to do this in India and beyond. They were amazed at the way we had grown in the challenging circumstances that India is home to.

HealthTec had never been a services company. Why did they want to acquire a dialysis provider in India? What was the real reason? Was it a desire to get into services? Did they think NephroPlus would provide them with the ideal platform to start services first in India and then to the rest of the developing world? HealthTec had tonnes of money. NephroPlus had the service DNA. Could this combination help propel HealthTec into services, something it had never done before?

Historically, few device manufacturers get into services. The other way round is probably rarer. The only example of the former that comes to mind is Fresenius. Founded in 1912 by Eduardo Fresenius as a pharmaceutical company, it started selling dialysis machines in 1966. Thirty years later, they merged with a dialysis services company called National Medical Care to form Fresenius Medical Care which, today, is the US's largest dialysis provider. This was one of the rare devices-to-services success stories.

I emailed Vikram about the call and we decided to talk the next day in the office. When we caught up the next day, we thought it would be worth pursuing this. This could be the opportunity to become part of a huge brand, which was also one of the most reputed in medical devices.

Start-ups are created mostly for one of three reasons. Build and grow organically, go public or exit to a strategic investor.

Entrepreneurs typically want to build something they are passionate about. What excites them is an unsolved problem or an underserved area that they are familiar with.

While all that some entrepreneurs want is to solve the problem and then scale the business, some entrepreneurs are more passionate about being entrepreneurs. Without too much attachment to the domain, they are excited about starting something from scratch and then growing and scaling it, and subsequently, exiting the business.

Exits can come about in two ways—an initial public offering (IPO) or a strategic exit. An IPO is where shares of the company are sold to the public who put in their money to become part owners of the company. A strategic exit is when a larger company acquires all or most shares of the company and becomes the majority owner of the company. There are some other minor variants to this but they are not so common.

In an IPO, it is imperative that the founders of the company continue to serve in their regular capacities as they understand the company like no one else. While some members of the founding team might liquidate some of their shares in order for them to get some money as a reward for bringing the company to this stage, it is usually ensured that they have enough ownership interest that the company continues to grow and generate value for new shareholders.

In a strategic exit, founders may cash some of their stock but are bound by a commitment clause where they are required to continue for a few years, at least, to ensure that the transition is smooth. Often, the acquiring company brings in its management expertise and the founders are usually not required to stay beyond a couple of years.

I looped Vikram into the email thread with Raj. Raj also looped in a broader team that looked after mergers and acquisitions.

Both teams signed confidentiality agreements. This was to ensure that they used the data we shared with them only for this engagement and did not share it with anyone who did not need to know. This was more of a legal requirement than of any real significance. Despite all the so-called watertight agreements drafted by expensive lawyers, information from these dockets is often leaked to various people. This was a risk everyone understood and took. Why companies continue to pay colossal sums of money to legal teams, I do not know. Maybe it was a deterrent against large-scale leaks.

We shared an initial set of data along with some projections for the coming months. We had several rounds of discussions.

At the end of it all, in November 2016, the HealthTec team came back with a letter of intent which had their offer. They mentioned the valuation they had arrived at. Of this, they would pay 60 per cent upfront on deal closure. They would pay the balance 40 per cent in two equal instalments at the end of one year each. They would prorate the balance to targets on the revenue (80 per cent weight) and the corporate EBITDA (20 per cent). So, if the company performed as well as we had projected, they would pay what we had agreed on, but if it did not, then they would pay less.

Over the next few weeks, we realized we had projected rather aggressively. While it had helped shore up the valuation, subsequent payouts at the end of the first and second years after the deal closure would be severely affected if we did not live up to those projections.

Rather sheepishly, we went back to them and said that we had relooked the numbers and found that they were too aggressive.

We sent them a revised set of numbers. This might have come as a surprise to them. They came back with a much lower valuation. They reduced the initial payment to 75 per cent and also made the targets for the later payouts more stringent.

We reviewed the situation. We realized that there was no competition for the acquisition. HealthTec knew they were the only ones in the game. We thought it would be good to get some competitors and hired an investment bank, Smiths*, to manage this acquisition transaction.

Investment bankers are a strange breed. They help manage such financial transactions. Mergers, acquisitions, investments by VCs and PE firms and so on. They make their money off other people's investments. These firms compete brutally with each other. The only place you would see similar levels of competitiveness is within the firm. People are often fired over a phone call and asked to take their belongings and leave the office instantly. This makes executives insecure, causing them to put in 100-hour weeks with no consideration for their personal lives.

They often make the transaction process efficient. Many transactions may not have happened had there been no banker. A layer gets added between the parties and this helps in the entire process. During negotiations, things can get tense and unpleasant. Having an experienced banker ensures egos don't get in the way and companies can conclude the transaction on merit. Most of the time.

They charge a lot. Each of the banking companies we worked with made more for a few months of work in one transaction than I did in my entire journey at NephroPlus—salary and stock included. That may not be a fair comparison, though. The banker was impacting the investors, who had enormous sums of money at stake. After a point, all the founders of the company were replaceable, apart from Vikram.

Smiths started off by reaching out to three other players who might be interested. Two of them already had a presence in India.

All of them expressed a keen interest. We created a virtual data room where our team started uploading documents containing the various sets of information that a potential buyer would need.

A virtual data room is some space on a server on the Internet where files meant to be shared for transactions of this nature are uploaded and interested parties are given access. It makes sharing sensitive data of the company straightforward. The companies that access the files do not know who the others accessing the files are.

The teams started accessing the data. While HealthTec already had most of the information they needed, the others started reviewing the information shared. Weeks passed by and this process continued.

One of the companies was too slow to move, and we felt they were not going anywhere.

One more had just acquired a dialysis company which was started around the same time as us. They had their hands full with this acquisition. They wanted exclusivity in the process and were unwilling to take part in a competitive bid. Exclusivity means a written guarantee that we would go ahead in this exercise only with them. We would not be able to engage with any other company. At the end of the exercise, if they came back with a ridiculously low valuation and other terms, we would be stuck with them. We were clear that this was impossible. We told them so and they opted out.

It was down to only two companies—HealthTec and I will call the other one Vital*.

* * *

On 7 February 2017, Vital got back with an offer. We declined the offer saying it was too low. We were quite upset that Smiths, the banker, had not guided their offer, especially since we already had an offer that was more than twice that amount. After we gave that feedback to Smiths, they spoke to the people at Vital.

On 22 February, Vital got back with a revised offer. They had upped their offer. They would pay a significant part of it upfront, and the rest of it at the end of one year, prorated to some targets on revenue and EBITDA. This prorated amount would have a floor of 75 per cent and a ceiling of 110 per cent. Which meant that even if we didn't meet any of the targets, the valuation would not go below 75 per cent and even if we exceeded the targets, the valuation would not go above 110 per cent. They did not give this offer in writing but communicated orally to Smiths, who checked with Vikram. Smiths indicated that there could be another Rs 50–60 crore that we could push them to do.

By this time, HealthTec had gone slow.[1] They did not explicitly say they would not take part. However, we could see signs that they were less interested than before. So, it was down to Vital.

Vital got back subsequently with a final non-binding offer with a certain enterprise valuation. The payouts would stay the same. We were quite happy with this offer and accepted.

Over the next several weeks, Vital would conduct diligence on our entire operations. A team of financial, legal and clinical experts would study our business. They would visit centres, evaluate our financial statements, look at our projections and evaluate if the data we provided was genuine or not.

This was a sensitive exercise. If our teammates got to know, they would panic. No one likes to be part of a company that is getting acquired. There is often a sense of insecurity when such an exercise happens. There is the fear of job losses, of changing dynamics, changing protocols, etc. Change is often unpleasant.

Vikram and I synced up on what the communication to the team should be and we decided on the following message:

'We will expand internationally this year. So, our prospective international JV partners, along with IFC, which is an expert in quality audits, will conduct thorough audits on our clinical care and operational capabilities. So, we need to be super buttoned up during this 45–60-day Audit period.'

Everyone bought the story.

The site visits and diligence exercise began and ended with no problems.

Our management team had a meeting with the senior leadership from Vital's Asia-Pacific team. We would make a presentation about the business to them. It turned out to be quite a spectacle. In a hotel in Hyderabad's HITEC City, we had booked a large meeting room that could seat about 100 people. The hall was set up with seating in the shape of a 'U' with the projector screen at one end. We took seats near the screen. We were geared up to make the presentation of our lives.

At the appointed time, the Vital team trooped in. It was an army of sorts. The top management from their Asia-Pacific team along with several members from their financial, operational and legal teams as well.

Vikram started the presentation by welcoming them and giving them an overview of the company and the journey till then. I then took over and talked them through the USP of the NephroPlus patient-centric care. Why we called our patients 'guests', Aashayein and the Olympiad. I also talked about clinical protocols and IT. We had a question-and-answer session after that. I thought it went off very well. Other management team members also presented.

That evening, some of Vital's senior folks and our management team met at the Dum Pukht at ITC Kakatiya. We had a wonderful conversation in an informal setting.

In a few days, Vikram got connected with Vital's CEO, Karl T*.

Karl T had become the CEO of Vital in the late 1990s. He had turned around the company to make it one of the US's largest dialysis provider chains. He was a rather colourful personality and came up with novel ways to motivate the team and make them feel part of a larger whole.

Karl and Vikram exchanged some emails. Karl hoped the deal would go through and asked Vikram if they could meet up. Vikram was travelling to the US in the last week of March and asked Karl's secretary to suggest a couple of time slots so that they could meet.

Karl had Vikram fly with him on his private jet from New York to the company's headquarters. Vikram also spent some time with other senior management folks from the company as well. They were trying to pitch hard to us, and Karl really wanted this to go through. In the conversation on the flight, Karl told Vikram that he was very keen that this deal came through and he had a lot of plans for Vikram to take on a larger role in Vital's Asia-Pacific operations. He hinted that he would like this to be like a reverse acquisition where while Vital was acquiring NephroPlus, the NephroPlus management would play a larger role in the Asia-Pacific operations of Vital.

The impression Vikram got from the multiple conversations he had with the team at Vital's headquarters was that the management was not happy with the way the company was being managed in India. They were very impressed by the way we had built our company. They believed Vikram could steer the Asia-Pacific arm of Vital in a much more efficient manner than it was being run.

Vikram got back, and we had to wait for their offer confirmation in writing. Towards the end of May, we started getting an inkling that something was amiss. Vital did not adhere to the committed timelines of getting back with the final offer. The bankers kept following up. They kept delaying on one pretext or the other. The reason they gave us was that they were having internal discussions relating to certain items.

We were getting restless.

After a point, we decided that we shouldn't be waiting for their offer and putting everything else on hold. We decided that we would go back to our regular work. We would deal with the offer when it came. Vikram emailed the management team and followed that up with an email to the board. He said Vital was unlikely to revert so we should just not think about it and focus on growing the company. Everyone agreed.

We never heard back from them. What caused this change of mind? Was it because of our government projects? Was it some aspect of our protocols? We would never know.

It was an anti-climax. What started off with HealthTec trying to acquire us and then Vital jumping into the fray, ended up with neither of them finally going through. We realized that we had made some mistakes in this process. We should have been a little less aggressive in the initial estimates given to HealthTec. Another competitor in the acquisition race, other than Vital, towards the end, would also have helped. This was difficult to do in the circumstances, but Vital probably knew that they were the only ones and that gave them an edge in the negotiations. In any such race, having competitors is crucial. However smart the people leading the discussions may be, no one can win over basic human instincts of dealing with competition.

Some would question the wisdom of doing government projects. We believe that in a country like India, that is the only way a large number of people are going to get dialysis. If we are not part of this, then we will be left out. Access and affordability, as I have said earlier, are the two main problems in Indian healthcare. If you don't participate in government projects, you will not address either of these problems. Only if the government steps in, will you be able to set up dialysis centres in rural areas where there are no proper healthcare facilities. And the only way anyone can do dialysis for the poor is if the government pays the provider.

Vital's centres in India were priced higher than ours. There was a reason we had adopted a certain price model. Due to this, we had to ensure that we incurred no wasteful expenditure on things that did not make an actual contribution to clinical quality. We could not afford to do things that were being done simply due to tradition or inertia to change.

Vikram always says that India is like a wide-bottomed pyramid. Even a small increase in the price of dialysis would lead to several thousand patients being priced out of the market. In this situation, could we go on improving quality and increase the price? We could not improve quality and not increase the price. That would make the venture unsustainable. We were an investor-backed company. The investors cared more about financial returns and less about clinical quality. For them, quality was important so long as it yielded a measurable improvement in value.

We did the best we could and ensured we struck the right balance between price and quality. We proved that our quality was excellent. How can you measure the quality of something like dialysis? Outcomes. How does the offered dialysis impact the quality of life of the guests and the improvement in their health? How does it impact mortality?

In these outcomes, our numbers matched the best in the world. An analysis of our mortality numbers in 2017 showed that our five-year mortality was about 50 per cent. The US and Europe had figures very similar to ours. We were the only provider from India that was publishing clinical outcome data in reputed nephrology conferences around the world like the World Congress of Nephrology, European Renal Association and American Society of Nephrology. No other provider was even putting out their data. We were proud of our outcomes and showcased them with pride.

This setback—if you can call it that—was only temporary. We were back on track almost immediately. What happened soon after is the stuff of legend. We would eventually be vindicated.

* * *

We were at about 120 centres when we wound up discussions with Vital in July 2017. The first Olympiad had taken place in February 2015 in Hyderabad. We decided to do the second towards the end of October 2017. This time, we decide to do it in Delhi. The event went off very well. Like the first event, patients from all over the country attended and had an excellent time.

Things were going very well. We were adding centres at a consistent rate.

On the morning of 27 July 2018, I got a call from Vikram. He said he had got a call from Chinta Bhagat from Khazanah. Chinta told Vikram something very interesting.

But first some background.

Khazanah was a sovereign wealth fund management company owned by the Government of Malaysia. Khazanah and Mitsui, a Japanese investment company, along with DaVita Inc., were joint venture owners of DaVita Asia Pacific, DaVita's entity that ran all their centres in the Asia-Pacific region.

Now, news in the market was that DaVita had decided to exit from the India business because it could not run it efficiently. Financially, they were doing pretty badly. Huge corporate overheads and only twenty-two centres to run. They were just not able to scale.

Around that time, DaVita took a hard look at their India operations. It was just not working out. They realized they could never have a sizeable presence in India given the challenging circumstances the country offered. They also realized that they could not even get their own centres to conform to their global clinical standards. Apart from this, they also had challenges with their financials. Given all these problems, I am not surprised that they decided to quit.

DaVita was in talks with Fresenius, who had just acquired Sparsh Nephrocare, yet another dialysis network that started around the same time as we did. Apparently, the deal was almost done. However, after an initial attractive offer, Fresenius had come back with another that was revised downwards, a result of the due diligence process.

Something about the DaVita asset, or the fact that they were the only bidders, made Fresenius reduce their offer by a sizeable amount. DaVita was upset, and the investors were obviously not at all happy. Pravan Malhotra, the partner from IFC who was on our board, knew Chinta Bhagat very well. Chinta had been in touch with Vikram over the years since IFC invested.

Chinta reached out to Vikram and told him that there was a small window of opportunity if NephroPlus was interested in acquiring DaVita India. If we could quickly make an offer upwards of a certain number, there could be some action.

Intriguing, indeed!

Vikram quickly got in touch with crucial members in the management team and then the board of directors. Everyone was supportive. The key was a quick offer. Vikram asked for the financials of DaVita India and promised them that we would get back shortly.

DaVita had twenty-two centres. While this was a reasonable number, we learnt that their entire operation hinged on a few large accounts. Two centres in two of their hospitals contributed to more than half their countrywide business.

We were certain that their quality wouldn't be bad. One major challenge that comes up from such kinds of acquisitions is that the quality of the acquired asset often needs a lot of improvement. From what we had heard, Fresenius had these issues while integrating the Sparsh Nephrocare centres. This was not something that might have been a problem with the DaVita centres. We were sure of that.

This was an opportunity of a lifetime. We were the number one dialysis provider in the country. All the other pure-play dialysis players combined could not match us in terms of volume, number of patients or revenues. If we actually acquired DaVita, we would be unassailable for a long time in India. On the other hand, if we did not make an offer, it was likely that DaVita would sell to Fresenius who would then get into a threatening position. Fresh from the Sparsh Nephrocare acquisition, they had started becoming very aggressive in adding new centres and they would then come within striking distance of NephroPlus.

We quickly analysed the brief financials provided to us and, on 5 August 2018, made a binding offer for the DaVita asset. This was subject to the customary due diligence which would be compressed and completed in seven days. The offer was a certain multiple of their annual revenue. Similar deals at that time were attracting similar multiples.

Coming up with the value of any asset, be it in healthcare or otherwise, is more about gut feel and less about arithmetic. In this case, we were told anything upwards of a certain number was what would get us into the game. We wanted this asset. So, we had to just convince ourselves that a number slightly more than that number was a fair value for the business. Chances are that if they had said upwards of another number, smaller or bigger, we might have come up with a different number. And we would also have an Excel spreadsheet with calculations to back those numbers!

We expected nothing major to change in the due diligence. DaVita would pull out of negotiations with Fresenius because of our offer. They wanted a penalty should we not fulfil the binding offer at the end of due diligence. They wanted a US$1 million penalty. We settled for half that amount.

Both parties quickly signed the binding offer. The due diligence exercise started. Our teams visited their centres. The visits had to be discreet without revealing why we were there. Some of our teammates were assigned centres. A team of people worked on the documents and data they had provided. Usually, such acquisitions would have a due diligence period of several months. Here, we were trying to squeeze everything into seven days.

We had a brief management presentation where the senior management would answer all our questions. Shriram Vijaykumar, Aditya Singh Grewal and others from their team attended the meeting.

The visits were all done but some questions asked of the DaVita team remained unanswered at the end of the week. We requested that the time be extended. They could see that we were genuine and not indulging in delaying tactics. They readily agreed.

We finally sent the confirmation to them on 16 August. We would have a couple of months to actually draft a detailed agreement where we would buy all the shares of the company DaVita Care India Pvt. Ltd and wire the money for buying those shares to the current owners, DaVita Inc. There were several conditions that needed to be met by them for this to happen. So, the game was still on and nothing could be considered finalized until we completed the ultimate step.

There were several grey areas left to be ironed out, though. Some of their centres had seen dips in revenue recently. There were a couple of centres that had to be moved to alternate locations. We started working on a transition plan. This had a detailed plan on various items, such as informing the hospitals, the nephrologists and the staff, transitioning of operations, clinical protocols and so on.

The legal team was busy drafting the agreement. During this exercise, several aspects—some major but most minor—came up where the two teams did not agree. We scheduled a meeting on 27 and 28 August at Hyderabad's Westin Hotel to iron out the issues. Senior folks from their team and some from ours met.

Such discussions are often about the ego. Why should I give in to this? Why should we allow them to 'win'? Both sides are guilty of this. I often wonder why people state a position assuming that there will be some negotiation. Both sides keep things they care little about to be given in with a show of reluctance when they have an opportunity to get something they really need in return. Wouldn't life be much simpler if people clearly stated what they were willing to give and what they would not give, no matter what?

That would, however, render several people jobless and so, I do not think it will ever happen, especially in the world of M&A.

After the two-day-long discussion, there were four identified issues on which the two teams could not come to a resolution. Their team got back with reasonable solutions by the end of the month. We accepted those fixes.

On 1 November, we signed the share purchase agreement. We wired the money to them in a couple of days after that.

We decided on 5 November as the transition date. Management team members would go to each of the major centres and announce the acquisition. I would address the team at their headquarters.

Transitioning twenty-two centres from one company to another was something we had never done in the past. There were several sensitivities to be kept in mind. Whenever a company gets acquired, there is a lot of uncertainty in the minds of employees. Will they be fired? Will they undergo a pay cut? How will the culture of the company change?

I flew to Bengaluru and drove straight to the DaVita India office in Shantinagar. The teammates there had no clue what had happened. They were ushered to the terrace at around 11 a.m. as I walked over to the front of the gathering. They were wondering what was in store for them. I began.

'Friends, I am thrilled to announce that NephroPlus has, today, acquired DaVita India. I would like to take this opportunity to welcome all of you to the NephroPlus family. NephroPlus is India's largest dialysis network and we have . . .'

I assured them that their jobs would all remain intact provided they performed well. There was a lot of concern among the teammates. They asked several questions about salaries, the company structure and so on. Some teammates started crying. I fully understood. We broke for lunch where I interacted informally with them.

Similar interactions took place in the centres where our management teammates interacted with the centre staff.

We sent emails to all DaVita nephrologists and hospitals. I sent emails and printed letters to all DaVita patients. We issued a press release that was carried by all major newspapers. 'NephroPlus acquires DaVita Care India', the headline read.

The announcement caused tremors in the healthcare ecosystem in India. People were shocked that an Indian healthcare start-up had acquired the Indian operations of the second-largest dialysis provider in the world. Rarely, if ever, had such a thing happened before. This was a classic David and Goliath story.

A few years ago, even before DaVita had acquired NephroLife, Dev Roy, the founder of Nephrocare, had flown down to Hyderabad to speak to us. One of their investors had accompanied him. We had only three centres at that time. During lunch, he asked Vikram to sell our company to them. He lowered his voice and cocked his face while adding that if we did not sell, they would come to Hyderabad and undercut us so heavily that we would be forced to shut down the company. He then looked Vikram in the eye and said, 'We have deep pockets.'

Vikram responded with a wry smile and said they were most welcome to do that. That is the swag you need to succeed. Yes, we were the smaller player. But by no means were we less capable. Money is not the only thing you need to succeed. While they may have had deep pockets, we had the gumption to beat them at their own game.

Our ability backed our attitude. We did not make foolish plans. By trusting our abilities, we grew the network, working hard, using intuition and being honest with our mission. We genuinely wanted to better the experience of our guests. We really wanted them to feel better, to lead fulfilling lives. Money was not our primary motivation. We keep saying that we are not a charity and so it was important to grow sustainably. We could not price dialysis at throwaway prices. If we did that, we could barely make a difference to a few thousand lives.

By being a for-profit company, we can do intelligent things. We partner with the government to offer excellent quality dialysis to the poorest dialysis patients. We also give a much better experience to those who can afford this dialysis at our non-PPP centres. By being such a company, we can conduct events such as the Olympiad and Aashayein, offer holiday dialysis, dialysis-on-wheels, buttonhole needles, etc., among other things. Most of these initiatives do not yield any added profit or revenue for us.

Having said that, I am amazed by the work some of the charity dialysis centres around the country are doing. Thousands of patients are alive because of these centres. There is a need for them and us. Both can coexist side by side. I do not agree with those who criticize charities for various reasons. That several thousand patients benefit from them is a testament to the excellent work they are doing.

People who berate us as being too commercial should also realize that such kinds of services are impossible to provide without being for-profit. The sums of money required for a chain of dialysis centres of this size with the leeway to do things that may not directly result in monetary benefits are astronomical.

Individuals from a middle-class background, like the founders of NephroPlus, do not have that kind of money. The only way we can do this is by engaging investors and convincing them that they should invest in the company. These investors care more about financials than other aspects.

So, running the company becomes a fine balancing act. You need to do what's right, what's in keeping with the company's values while also making sure that the investors get a good return on their investment. There is no other way.

Sustainability becomes key. The company has to grow responsibly. At every stage, decisions are to be made. This balance between the guest and the investor comes back to test us. We cannot sway either way. We have to be balanced.

I am confident we could do that most of the time. We are not perfect though. Sometimes, we might have swerved too much to one side or the other.

I spoke to Vikram that evening on the way back to the airport, reminding him of the Dev Roy conversation many summers back. We patted each other on the back. That day was the pinnacle of our lives.

* * *

Epilogue

'I shall be telling this with a sigh
Somewhere ages and ages hence:
Two roads diverged in a wood, and I—
I took the one less travelled by,
And that has made all the difference.'

—Robert Frost

From one five-bed centre way back in 2010 in a quiet bylane of Hyderabad's Banjara Hills to become India's largest dialysis centre network, we had come a long way. The progress was organic. Starting with a single centre, we then did the multicentre model. Then, the multicity model. Next, we did multiple states in the same zone within the county. Then we moved to the north. And then, other zones in the country.

The next logical step was to go out of the country. That would be the next challenge for the entire team. Could we replicate our model, even with a few changes, to suit the local dynamic in other similar countries?

We set up a centre in Birgunj, Nepal, but it was so close to our centres in Bihar and so similar that we did not feel like it was another country.

We started looking at other international opportunities. There were several inquiries from countries who had heard about our story and our tremendous success in setting up dialysis centres focused on the patient experience and quality, despite the constraints of a developing country and lack of affordability among patients. People from countries in Africa, the Middle East, South Asia and South-east Asia had reached out to us. It was a mix of dialysis providers, governments and companies in healthcare who wanted to set up dialysis centres.

We explored several options. We decided to start with a country that could be reached by a direct flight in less than four hours from India. This was from an ease of operations perspective. Indonesia seemed to be interesting. The government there had just launched a universal healthcare scheme and was offering dialysis to all its citizens. This was key for a developing country. Citizens in such countries can rarely afford to pay for expensive, chronic treatments like dialysis and state-sponsored healthcare is the only solution.

We tried setting up joint ventures with local companies on two occasions. Things did not work out and we had to shelve plans both times.

In the second half of 2020, we acquired a majority stake in a six-centre dialysis network in the Philippines called Royal Care Dialysis Centres founded by Sunil Chellani, a person of Indian origin who had settled in the Philippines several years ago. This was our first genuine international expansion. Our aim was to slide into operations smoothly and not cause any sudden or major changes. We needed to respect the cultural differences between India and the Philippines. We just sent two people to do a gradual integration. Yet another example of Vikram's foresight and mature leadership!

We grew the Philippines network by acquiring other dialysis centres and at the time of this writing are at thirteen centres.

The government of the Republic of Uzbekistan (formerly part of the USSR) wanted to set up a PPP project where a private operator ran dialysis operations that was paid for by the government. They floated a tender which we won even though we were pitted against top dialysis companies in the world like Fresenius and Diaverum. We run four centres there including a massive 160-machine centre in the capital, Tashkent.

Believing we are best placed to disrupt markets where a dialysis session is priced less than US$100, we continue to look for opportunities to expand internationally. We have established ourselves as the leading dialysis provider in India, which is as challenging a market as it can get. We will need to explore various models—joint ventures with local partners as we did in the Philippines or set up things on our own as we are doing in Uzbekistan.

New challenges will come. We may make mistakes. We will learn from them. Our solid presence in India will act as a cushion. There are several countries with similar problems as India. Our model should help us solve these problems.

While we found moving to different parts of India difficult in the early days of the company, this move to other countries will be several times more difficult. There will be different laws, regulations, cultures and governments to deal with.

It will be critical to stick to the basics and focus on providing what our guests love about us—standardized, guest-centred care. That should help us grow in other countries in the coming years.

NephroPlus has given me the opportunity of a lifetime to do something I am passionate about. Providing dialysis services to patients and changing their lives is more than I could ever have asked. I often get emails from our guests expressing their gratitude for the services we offer. They also comment on how they have been inspired by my journey from being a dialysis patient to a co-founder of a large dialysis centre network. They derive hope from my story and are motivated to achieve their dreams as well. I have got several emails and have spoken to several guests who, after reading my story, have gone back to work, have started up their businesses again, or resumed forgotten hobbies.

When I hear such things, I feel grateful for my life. Given the circumstances, I cannot complain about how things have turned out. I might complain about the circumstances themselves, but not the eventual outcome.

I have had several challenges in life. And every time, I have been able to find a way out. When the kidney transplant did not work, I found out about and opted for PD. When PD failed, I took on home HD.

The ideal outcome for me would be a successful kidney transplant. However, until the drug eculizumab (brand name Soliris, manufactured by Alexion Pharmaceuticals, acquired by Astra Zeneca in 2021) or an alternative becomes available in India, the chances of a successful kidney transplant are less than 5 per cent. The drug is one of the most expensive in the world. In most developed countries, it is funded by the government or by insurance companies. The company does not consider India as a market because of poor affordability and abysmal government spending on healthcare.

Until something drastic changes on this front, I will have to continue to be on dialysis.

There are several challenges that come up in the dialysis process as well. Problems with my fistula requiring a minor procedure, problems with the dialysis machine, the water treatment plant and problems with technicians who come to help with my dialysis.

I get overwhelmed by these problems, sometimes. I find it difficult to shoulder this burden. While my parents are there to help with some of this, there is a limit to what they can do.

These times are the most difficult. I believe I can deal with being on dialysis for the rest of my life, provided there are no other problems. But that is not how life is, right? I have all the other problems that others have, plus I have to deal with the dialysis.

Sometimes I feel, what is the point of all this? What is the point of labouring so hard to make my treatment work? Do I have something to look forward to? Is there something that makes my life and all the struggle worth it?

This feeling is exacerbated by seeing everyone around me leading normal lives. They don't have to worry about bone pain due to fluctuating parathyroid hormone levels. They don't have to make sure there's a good dialysis centre at the destination they travel to. They can do more than overnight trips even when there's no dialysis centre there. No worrying about fistula problems. No worrying about heart function. What a carefree life!

And yet, when I look around me, I find people messing up their lives with the most trivial and inconsequential things. Meaningless pursuits of power and wealth.

Of pandering to egos.

Or overindulging in stimulants.

Or letting work take over life to an extent that they lose sight of what they're working for. Work-related stress is a major problem for so many people.

When I see healthy people messing up their lives, I feel thankful that I live a more mindful life. I am grateful for the awakening my kidney disease has caused. This has enabled me to lead a full life. Not letting one single aspect take over my life, I make sure I do multiple things.

These days, I bake sourdough bread. I spent several weekends experimenting to figure out the best way to make good idlis. I write a blog, and have taken online courses in biostatistics and the statistical software, R. I recently wrote and passed an exam that certified me as a dialysis technician by the reputed BONENT in the US.

Particular about my general physical fitness, I swim or walk or cycle four to five times a week and do strength training four times a week.

In my community, I teach kids about life values and the Jain religion in a manner that is devoid of dogma. I meditate and journal every morning.

And all this, after putting in a full day's work for NephroPlus, which has its own pressures. I lead a full life.

I make my life worth living despite all the problems that dialysis and long-term kidney failure bring with them. These are the things that make all these problems worthwhile. I like to fill my life with so many things I enjoy that I look forward to the rest of my life while I am not hooked to the machine.

When someone gets diagnosed with kidney failure, there are two possible ways they can react.

In the first way, people simply go along with what happens. Like a boat without oars that traverses with the flow of water. Currents take it from side to side. It just goes along.

The other way is when people take control of the boat. Despite whatever currents might come and however strong they may be, they try to steer the boat in the direction they want to go in.

I never considered the first option, even for a fleeting moment. The second option came naturally to me. I had to be in control. There would be no giving up.

That was the logical choice. To me, quality of life was paramount. I needed to lead a normal life or as close to that as I could get. Every time I had a problem, I tried to figure out how I could get back my life. That was the only motivation. Nothing else. Normality is the only thing I desired. Everything else followed.

Some people believe you need courage to deal with such a disease. To me, that sounds rather bombastic. What courage? It is only the desire to be free from pain and suffering. We are all born with that instinct.

NephroPlus has helped provide the *ikigai* of my life. Ikigai, a Japanese concept, means the higher purpose of one's life. Ikigai, many studies have shown, adds years to one's life. Working towards a higher cause, something more than the individual, makes life worth living and adds happiness to your days. I am eternally grateful to Vikram for enabling this. Without him and his brilliant vision, planning, intellect, networking and courage, this would never have happened.

When I see that we have brought standardized, quality-focused dialysis to thousands of patients, I feel that we have achieved something phenomenal. When people want to travel, they often decide to go only if there is a NephroPlus centre there. That is the level of trust we have established among dialysis patients (both within and outside NephroPlus).

We are the only provider in India and much of the developing world that publishes patient outcomes in reputed international journals and conferences. This is because we are proud of our outcomes.

Outcomes, to me, are the ultimate testament of our work. That is the end result. How has our dialysis impacted the lives of our guests? Outcomes provide an answer to that question in an objective manner. Not some fuzzy statement that screams 'good dialysis'. But a reproducible, verifiable, number-based answer. We can proudly say we have the best outcomes in the country.

This gives us tremendous satisfaction. All our hard work, all the stress that Vikram and I and the entire team have undertaken over the past decade and more has been worth it.

We continue to expand both within India and outside. Our core values remain the same. Our guest-centric DNA is the key. We need to make sure that remains. Right down to the last mile of service delivery. People will come and go. But this DNA must not change. No scope for genetic mutations here!

* * *

Acknowledgements

I would like to thank early reviewers of the book including my dad, my brothers, Prasan and Karan, and my mother, an invaluable source of strength for our family and an inspiration to many.

I would also like to thank Vikram Vuppala for making NephroPlus happen and for his inputs on the book—correcting mistakes, refining some parts, and for his incessant support in whatever I did. Vikram is the reason I found my calling and have been able to do something so close to my heart. Vikram is also largely responsible for the success of NephroPlus.

Sandeep Gudibanda, my co-founder's continuous insistence to write this book has been instrumental in my getting started. Sandeep was also instrumental in introducing me to the literary agent who helped with the publishing process.

My school, the Hyderabad Public School, Begumpet in Hyderabad, has shaped me into the person I am today. And for that, I am eternally grateful. To the school, the teachers, my fellow students. Mrs Marien Oommen, my English teacher, has played an understated, yet humungous part in this journey. She instilled in me a love for the written word that eventually led me to blog and then write this book. As I wrote every sentence, I made sure

I checked for spelling and grammar, lest Mrs Oommen make a red mark in her copy of the book.

Ramesh Karra, also from my school, reviewed an early draft of the book and gave some very helpful feedback for which I shall remain grateful.

I am indebted to author Moitreyee Bhadhuri, someone I have never met. I have only spoken to her on the phone. Her sage advice and words of encouragement were incredibly useful to this fledgling author with no experience in the world of publishing.

I would also like to thank R. Gopalakrishnan for his help in the publishing journey. Without his support, this book would not have been published.

I am thankful to Kanishka Gupta for being interested in my book, to Radhika Marwah of Penguin for believing in the book from the start and to Ralph Rebello and his team for patiently editing the draft.

I am deeply indebted to all the doctors who treated me over the years, giving me the best possible care and ensuring I have managed to beat the odds. They have always involved me in decisions pertaining to my care, which was one of the most important factors for a good quality of life. Special thanks to Dr Girish Narayen, Dr Rajasekhara Chakravarthi, Dr P.C. Gupta and Dr Anuj Kapadia for all their care over the years.

Thanks also to all the dialysis technicians and nurses, especially Jayaram Reddy, Venkatraman G. and Guruvulu who have helped with my home haemodialysis.

Finally, I would like to thank the entire NephroPlus team for being part of this journey, all our dear guests who have entrusted us with their lives, all our nephrologist and hospital partners for all your support through the years and most importantly, our investors who believed in our vision to reshape the way dialysis was done in India and beyond.

Notes

Chapter 1. The Dawn That Wasn't

1 Mistaking my blood cells for foreign bodies, my immune system started attacking them. Several million of my blood cells were being broken into fragments every minute. This attack compromised the entire circulatory system in my body. My haemoglobin levels started falling. My platelet count started falling. I was becoming anaemic.

  In the human body, blood flows through the cells of the kidney for purification. The trouble is, the kidneys cannot discern fragmented blood cells from healthy cells. When these fragments went into the cells of my kidneys, they started affecting their functioning as well. It was as if the blood cell fragments were getting lodged in the kidneys and blocking their normal functioning as well.

2 The hospital staff took me to the operation theatre where a urologist performed an hour-long surgery where two pieces of a plastic pipe were inserted into my hand (into two veins) for easy access to the blood. They connected the two pieces outside the arm using a smaller piece of pipe which they fastened using a plaster.

3 I learnt later this was called a femoral access.

4 ATN is one of the most common causes of Acute Kidney
   Injury (AKI) and may be caused by drugs that are toxic for the
   kidneys. ATN may also occur due to low blood pressure and
   other causes.

5 The reason, as I would find out much later, was that the body's
   complement system, which had a very important role in the
   immune mechanism, used a protein called Complement Factor
   H. This factor was present in the blood's plasma. In many aHUS
   patients, this Factor H misbehaves. This is because of a genetic
   mutation that has messed up parts of the gene that dictate the
   performance of this Factor H. Now, if you give plasma from
   a donor who has the right genetic code for Factor H, it might
   help to bring back the complement system to normal. Even
   better was to remove the 'bad' Factor H containing plasma
   from the patient's body and replace it with 'good' Factor H
   containing plasma. This may just bring the complement system
   back to normal.

6 This was a simple procedure through which they would put in a
   small device that would clear up the entire passage and remove
   the clots.

7 Haemolytic Uremic Syndrome (HUS) usually manifests with
   three characteristics: thrombocytopenia (low platelet counts),
   haemolytic anaemia (low haemoglobin with fragmented red
   blood cells) and kidney failure (elevated serum creatinine,
   among others). HUS can be typical or atypical.

   Typical HUS is almost always preceded by bloody
   diarrhoea, and all the damage usually reverses in a week or ten
   days with supportive therapy. Typical HUS is mostly seen in
   toddlers. It rarely recurs. Mortality is very low.

   Atypical HUS is not preceded by bloody diarrhoea. Most
   of the damage is irreversible. A lot of patients end up with
   kidney failure. Several die.

Chapter 3. A Flawed Solution

1 Prior to 1954, several unsuccessful attempts were made at transplanting a kidney from one human to another. The first successful attempt was made in Boston when a kidney was transplanted into Richard Herrick from his identical twin brother, Ronald Herrick. Being identical twins, the problem of immunosuppression would almost be negligible.

The human body has evolved to learn how to fight everything that is not a part of it. This mechanism enables it to fight off invading bacteria and viruses and helps protect the body against the deleterious effects of the organisms.

A kidney transplant involves taking a kidney from the donor and placing it inside the recipient. For the recipient, the new kidney is a foreign body. It treats it like any bacterium or virus and attacks it. It tries to protect itself from what it considers an invader. If this immune response is allowed to work, then the new kidney would be destroyed by the body.

Since they were identical twins, Richard Herrick's body did not identify his brother's kidney as a foreign body. The transplant lasted eight years before Richard Herrick died.

When the donor and recipient are not identical twins, however, the recipient's immune system becomes a major hurdle. Scientists came up with a solution in 'immunosuppression' which suppresses the mechanism by which the body protects itself from foreign bodies. This causes the immune system to not recognize the kidney as an outsider and allows the kidney to lead a happy life within the body.

One side effect of immunosuppression is that the body cannot fight even regular infections and great care needs to be taken by the patient to not expose themselves to sources of infection. Immunosuppression evolved over the years and several drugs became available with distinct advantages and disadvantages.

2 Sahay M., 'Men Are from Mars, Women Are from Venus: Gender Disparity in Transplantation', *Indian J. Transplant* 2019; 13:237–9.

3 They found the mutation in the Complement Factor H gene. I had a hybrid gene called CFH/CFHR1.

4 The complement system of the body is responsible for fighting infections. It comprises three pathways: the classical pathway, the alternate pathway and the lectin pathway. For people who have this genetic mutation, uncontrolled activation of the alternative complement pathway occurs, making the immune system of the body attack its own blood cells, causing them to fragment and eventually cause kidney failure.

Why does a kidney transplant cause this complement activation? Any activity that is like a foreign body entering the body can cause this. The new kidney that is being placed in the body is a foreign body. The body does not recognize it as its own. It treats it like an outside body. It considers the kidney as something dangerous and triggers the immune system. The mechanism to control the immune system is defective and the checks and balances that should work, do not work. This causes recurrence of the disease.

The same thing had happened in the past when I had taken the vaccinations. A vaccine introduces cells that are like the organism that it protects against. This causes the body's immune system to react and produce antibodies or cells that fight the infection. Through this process, the body learns how to fight the infection when it might occur in the future.

However, in people with my mutation and other such mutations, the mechanism to fight the infection goes out of control and starts attacking the body's own cells. This results in kidney failure.

Chapter 4. Some Peace at Last

1 The peritoneal cavity is a space that exists between the inner lining of the abdomen and the lining of the stomach and intestines. The two linings (each called a peritoneum) are semi-permeable. This nature of the peritoneum causes it to become a potential membrane for dialysis.

2 Like most things in science, it was a gradual process. It wasn't like suddenly someone realized that they could use the peritoneum for dialysis overnight. In the late nineteenth century, three scientists, Clark, Orlo and Wegner, found that infusing a solution into the peritoneum in animals increased its volume. Why they were experimenting with this, we do not know. However, that truly was the seed for this magical process. Subsequently, a scientist called Babb demonstrated bidirectional transport through the peritoneum. In 1978, Popovich and Moncrief started using glass bottles for their patients in a technique similar to the one being used today. Oreopoulos from Toronto Western Hospital, however, was the first to use plastic bags like we use them today and was instrumental in the widespread adoption of peritoneal dialysis.

3 A surgeon places a catheter in the abdomen with the tip residing inside the peritoneal cavity. They leave the other end outside the body. They infuse sterile dextrose solution through this catheter into the peritoneal cavity and the fluid dwells in the cavity for around three to six hours, during which excess toxins and fluid in the blood diffuse through the peritoneal membrane into this fluid. At the end of the dwell period of three to six hours, this fluid becomes saturated with toxins and fluid and can no longer take any additional load. They then drain it out by opening the outer end of the catheter into a drain bag. Fresh fluid is then infused again, and

this cycle is repeated three to four times a day. It takes about thirty to thirty-five minutes each time.

4 We did a test called the Peritoneal Equilibrium Test. This test determines the rate of transfer of solutes across the peritoneal membrane. The test would show whether I was a 'low transporter' or a 'high transporter'. High transporters were more suited to PD using a cycler because the dwell periods were shorter on a cycler and you could get more out in a shorter duration. Low transporters are more suited to manual exchanges because the dwell periods are longer and you need the extra time so that you could get rid of more toxins. My test returned a result of 'low average', which did not rule out a cycler but meant that I may not get very good dialysis. Still, we went ahead with automated PD at night using a cycler because of the convenience it offered.

Chapter 6. Taking the Uncharted Path

1 There are many cases where technicians find it difficult to cannulate a fistula and have to prick multiple times to get the needle into the vein in a manner that ensures the required flow of blood for dialysis to be effective.

Chapter 7. I Had a Dream

1 My primary kidney disease, atypical haemolytic uremic syndrome (aHUS), causes the body's complement system (a part of the body's immune system) to go into overdrive and attack organs such as the kidney causing kidney failure. Researchers invented a drug, eculizumab, which would inhibit the complement system and prevent it from attacking organs, thus preventing kidney failure. The drug needs to be administered fortnightly thereafter. In aHUS patients who did

not have access to eculizumab when aHUS first occurred and whose kidneys failed, aHUS is known to recur even if they have a kidney transplant, causing the transplanted kidney to be attacked and the kidney to fail. However, if eculizumab is administered a few hours before the kidney transplant and fortnightly thereafter, the chances of the kidney working increase to more than 95 per cent.

2 The parathyroid hormone secreted by the parathyroid glands in the body has one primary function: to control the level of calcium in the blood. Calcium plays a very important role in the body. Apart from being essential for maintaining the health of bones and teeth, contraction of muscles, release of neurotransmitters, regulation of heartbeat and clotting of blood are all dependent on calcium. When calcium levels in the body fall, the glands release more parathyroid and this hormone leaches calcium from the bones and releases it into the blood. When the level of calcium rises, the amount of the hormone released reduces to reduce calcium levels.

Chapter 9. Differentiating Ourselves

1 Patrick Tang, MPH, 'A Brief History of Peer Support: Origins', http://peersforprogress.org/pfp_blog/a-brief-history-of-peer-support-origins/

Chapter 10. Brick by Brick

1 'The Economics of Dialysis in India,' https://www.indian jnephrol.org/article.asp?issn=0971-4065;year=2009;volume= 19;issue=1;spage=1;epage=4;aulast=Khanna

2 'Ironman Triathlon', https://en.wikipedia.org/wiki/Ironman_ Triathlon

Chapter 12. The Winner Takes It All

1 At the time of writing this, HealthTec's dialysis machine, which promises to use very little water, is still under development. They have a development centre in India.

* Name has been changed to protect the identity.